Dear
Senthuran

ALSO BY AKWAEKE EMEZI
AVAILABLE FROM
RANDOM HOUSE LARGE PRINT

The Death of Vivek Oji

Dear Senthuran

◆ A BLACK SPIRIT MEMOIR ◆

AKWAEKE EMEZI

RANDOM HOUSE
LARGE PRINT

The following have been previously published, in different form,
in these publications: "Nowhere/Dear Katherine" in
212 Magazine (2017); "Fire/Dear Jahra," as "Sometimes the
Fire Is Not Fire," in a literary supplement published by
Olisa.tv (2015); "Mutilation/Dear Eugene," as "Transition,"
at **The Cut** (2018). "Masks/Dear Maki," as "In Lagos," in
Dazed (2018); "Canon/Dear Daniel," as "Writers of Color Are
Making Their Own Canon," at **BuzzFeed** (2018); "Maps/Dear
Toni," as "This Letter Isn't For You," at **Them** (2019).

Cover design by Grace Han
Cover art by Ruby Onyinyechi Amanze

The Library of Congress has established a
Cataloging-in-Publication record for this title.

ISBN: 978-0-593-41423-1

www.penguinrandomhouse.com/large-print-format-books

FIRST LARGE PRINT EDITION

Printed in the United States of America

10 9 8 7 6 5 4 3 2 1

This Large Print edition published in accord with
the standards of the N.A.V.H.

TO MY BELOVED SPIRITBAE,
THE PROPHET AND SEER,
MY FAVORITE VOID.

TO THOSE OF US
STILL WITH ONE FOOT
ON THE OTHER SIDE.

Nowhere | Dear Katherine

It is the middle of June.

The Black Sea is turquoise, stained by blooms of phytoplankton and polished with undulating mirrors, sunlight reflecting in ripples over the water. I stand on a tumble of rocks, holding an empty plastic water bottle and listening as the waves spit foam into the quiet of the morning. Seagulls wheel and yell against the sky. A magician I am falling in love with has asked me to bring him back a drop or two of the sea, this specific sea, the one I am close to. I meant to retrieve it—this seapiece—when I went swimming the other day, but I forgot. Instead I stood thigh deep in a cloud of green algae for an hour, my calves numb and my back burning. None of it made me feel as if I was anywhere.

Perhaps it was the traveling, airports, and rough blue seats blurring into safety announcements, or the cities—white chocolate drizzled on a waffle at a picnic in Johannesburg, an Orthodox monk walking through a thunderstorm in Sofia, a little girl with afro-puffs selling homemade lemonade in Brooklyn. Maybe it was the homelessness—a terminated lease in Trinidad, too many guest rooms in too many countries. They say the word **nomad** like it has a rough glamour, but in my mouth it is jet-lagged, wearing a sheet mask with fifteen minutes left, a draped attempt to fix its dehydration.

I don't even mind anymore.

The state of my body matches that of my mind—floating, tripped, and suspended amid clouds, crashing down into borders, lonely. Nowhere seems real; all the people are constructs. I have stopped fighting detachment and started learning how to sink into it instead.

Rumi suggests being dead to this world and alive only to God; in Sozopol, a former monk leans across a dinner table with bright stained-glass eyes and tells me about the types of nothingness in Buddhism. I tell him that my search for somewhere to be is really a search for self, and the only self I feel at home with is one that doesn't exist, not anymore, one that's been taken apart, whipped into dust.

I tie back my hair, so it doesn't interfere with my eyes, and start climbing down toward the sea. My sneakers slide slowly over the wet rock and I drop my legs into crevices, press my palm against outcrops. The rest of the land grows higher and higher as I sink. The sea pulls. I could see how people would try to lose themselves in it, when the detachment gets too strong, when the urge to be nowhere becomes an action. I unscrew the cap from the bottle I'm carrying and crouch on a rock, dropping my hand and waiting for the surf to wash it full. I feel utterly alone. The water is clear inside the faint blue plastic. I should leave—I have buses and planes to catch—but this curve of nothing feels too right, so I sit there for a long time.

I text the magician, tell him about the way the sun turns the rocks into cradles and clothes-racks. Perhaps, with time, if I waited here long enough, I could dissolve into foam and be withdrawn into something vaster than my immediate body.

I want to be nothing, nowhere.

The magician texts me back. **I too am turquoise,** he says, **stained by phytoplankton.**

Fire | Dear Jahra

Kerosene burns nearly everything.

Growing up, our house was sometimes invaded by soldier ants, rivers of red, clacking bodies that ran over our windowsills and bit us with thoroughness. We soaked newspaper in kerosene to make torches and burnt the ants back, singeing our carpets and bathtubs. The price of petrol kept climbing, so we transferred all our cooking over to the small green kerosene stove and watched as the pots blackened. In the dry season, we raked dead leaves into a pile next to the borehole that didn't work, sprinkled some kerosene, and dropped a flame. I remember being amazed at how a little wetness could lead to such fire. My little sister and I danced around the blaze until we got called in and scolded for getting smoke in our hair.

When you try to burn a person, it is cheaper to use kerosene instead of petrol.

I spent my entire childhood in Aba, a commercial town in the south of Nigeria, where both my siblings were born. When I came back to the country after leaving for college, I knew from my first circling of the Lagos crowd that the location of my childhood could serve as ammunition against people who thought I didn't belong, that I wasn't Nigerian enough. No one argues with Aba. It was my best card—better even than being born in Umuahia, where my father and grandfather were born. It made me "authentic" in a way that was absolute; you couldn't question if someone who grew up in Aba was a "real" Nigerian, even though it didn't match what people assumed my background was. I looked and smelled too foreign, even down to my blood, so I must have grown up outside Nigeria or, at the very least, spent all my holidays abroad.

The truth felt like a story. I wanted to tell them how we never had running water, how cockroach eggs gelled into the egg grooves of the fridge door, how the concrete over the soakaway broke and stayed open, the rancid smell becoming part of our air. We longed after green apples that were too expensive, three for a hundred naira swinging in a plastic bag, and we knew the intimate taste of ketchup smearing red on white bread, the cheap oiliness of margarine mixed into boiled rice, the accompanying shame. I didn't say any of this. I just smiled and listened to the jokes about how Aba people can make and sell a fake version of anything, even a glass of water.

I grew up with piles of books to read, bought secondhand from the post office on Ikot-Ekpene Road or sent from our cousins in London or pulled from my parents' separate collections. While the town was burning from the riots, my sister and I believed in invisible fairies, pixies hiding in our backyard. We had cats spilling over our carpets, a dog with raw,

bleeding ears, and several Barbie dolls sent
from Saudi Arabia, where my mother had
moved in 1996. I didn't know that I'd never
live with her again. When our turkeys got
fowl pox, we caught them and pinned them
under our feet and learned that you could
treat the pox with palm oil. When the dogs
got maggots, we learned that applying careful pressure to the sore made them fall, white
and wriggling, to the sand. We learned not
to touch your mouth after handling bitterleaf,
or touch your eyes after peeling yam, because
the first ruins your tongue and the itch of
the second can blind you. We mimicked the
priests during Mass at CKC, whispering under
our breath when we were meant to be silent.
**Deliver us, Lord, from every evil, and grant
us peace in our day.** On the drive home, we
passed the familiar heap of decomposing bodies dumped outside the teaching hospital, their
loss loud in the air. We played in the car. We
stayed children.

After a pickup truck shattered my sister's leg
in 1995, my father forbade us to ride okadas,
saying that the roads were too dangerous. I
disobeyed often, leaning into the wind and

raising my heels away from the burning exhaust so my slippers wouldn't melt. The first time I climbed on one, my best friend called out my name, distracting me, and I burned the inside of my leg on the metal. She made a face. "Look out for the exhaust pipe," she said. By the time I went to school the next day, my burn had bubbled up and split. I packed it with powder and two types of iodine, till it was ugly and crusted in purples and reds. Eventually it scarred flat, and I learned to climb onto motorcycles from the other side.

After I burned my sister's left thigh, I learned that hot wounds always bubble reliably, whether you make them with metal or, in her case, water. We were all sitting to breakfast at the dining table one morning, the way my mother liked it when she was there, with the Milo and sugar and powdered milk and everything laid out. I reached over to grab the handle of the hot-water flask, but our brother hadn't screwed the top back on properly, so when the flask toppled over, it spilled a steaming river over my sister's school uniform, scalding her leg. She jumped up screaming and ran into the parlor, everyone rushing to her while I apologized frantically. I think they cracked a raw egg over the burn, viscous and yellow. It was the second time I'd seen the skin of her leg do unnatural things. The first was when the pickup had dragged her down Okigwe Road, but her skin had opened differently then, more intricately, chopped up by white bone screaming out of the pulpy red. My best friend's father fixed it. I learned that humans are meat.

Bodies in the sun smell unbearable after a week because meat goes bad, but they smell even worse a week later. One evening, it rained while I was walking back home, and in the flooded water of Faulks Road, I learned that a dead body will float and even bob. I learned that brains were gray before I was eleven, from the tarmac of Brass Junction, from the cracked calabash of what was a person's head. We looked at it every day on our way to school, holding our breath as we drove through the junction and turned left on Aba-Owerri Road, heading toward Abayi. I learned that we can bear much more than we predict.

When the armed robberies in Aba got too

bad, to the point where you could report one to the police and they would just make sure to avoid the area, a team of young vigilantes formed in response. They called themselves the Bakassi Boys. Their headquarters were in Ariaria Market, and we often saw them as we returned from school, their vehicles whistling down the road. They dangled out of car windows and off bus roofs, waving machetes and guns streaming with red and yellow strips of cloth.

They killed and burned thieves, hacking them with machetes, throwing a tire and that faithful kerosene over them, then leaving the corpses out as warnings and reminders. No one dared to remove the bodies until it was allowed. When I was fourteen, we went to Malaysia to see my grandparents, and I told one of my cousins about the Bakassi Boys. "That's terrible, that they're killing people," she said as we walked on the beach. I looked at her like she didn't make sense. Even our own state governor had allowed the killings— just like he allowed the riots in 2000 after the massacre of Igbos in Kaduna, after they stacked our dead in lorries and sent them back to us.

Looking back, I think about how casual taking a life was, how young I must have been.

I learned other things in Aba: that a mother you see once a year is a stranger, no matter how much you cry for her in the long months when she's gone. That if my father is a man who will wield a machete at the NEPA worker who came to check the meter, then I cannot tell him what our neighbor who took my sister to the hospital after the pickup accident did to me, because at twelve I am entirely too young for that kind of blood on my hands. They treated that neighbor like a hero; he called my sister his little wife for years. We can, I promise you, bear much more than we predict.

I told a friend some of this during a lunch in Lagos—not the parts about myself, just about the bodies and the curfews and the ritual kidnappings they called Otokoto and the time they burnt down the mosque and killed every Muslim person they could find, murdering three hundred Northerners in the two

days after the lorries arrived with the bodies from Kaduna, when we got five days off
from school and stayed at home and saw the
ashes in front of the Customs House. I told
her how a classmate had joked with me then
that I should be careful. "You know you re-
semble a Northerner," he said. I told her about
the rumors of a Muslim man who could pass
for Igbo, and so when they came for him, he
joined the mob and killed his own people to
stay alive, to prove he was one of us. I told
her about the woman next door, whose gate-
man was a shoemaker from the North, how
she hid him and his five-year-old son in their
boysquarters. When the child heard the noise
in the street, he tried to run out to see what
it was, but she caught him and beat him and
sent him back. He was five. We shared an avo-
cado tree with their compound.

We were sitting in Freedom Park when I
said these things, and my friend stared at me
the whole time, horrified. "You're making that
up," she said. "Are you serious?"

"It was Aba in the nineties," I reminded her.
"I thought everyone in Nigeria grew up like

this." I hadn't expected her to be surprised. She was Nigerian too, after all, and older than me. Surely, she'd seen worse things.

"No, everyone did not grow up like that!" She was agitated. "Why don't you write about this?"

I shrugged because it was just death and Aba was just Aba. None of it had seemed worth writing about. I could hear how the stories sounded when I said them out loud, dark like old blood, like I was supposed to be traumatized, different, like something in me, perhaps my innocence, should've caught a whiff of kerosene and gone crackly and black, too, smoking away like suya edges. Except I felt like nothing had happened. In college, I had a friend from Serbia who wouldn't even talk about the things he'd seen. I had a girlfriend in New York who'd spent years of her childhood in the middle of the war in Liberia. We know that life churns on, bloody and normal, as sacrilegious as that sounds.

After I wrote **Freshwater,** I had to reconcile with the fact that I'm not even human. What does that mean about how I see life, or, more important, death? I am thinking of the place I grew up in and the self that was formed there, the version of me who knows that a body is meat but also someone's child. I am thinking of how the darkness can live inside your memories, even as a town goes aflame twenty years ago.

Sometimes the fire is not fire. Sometimes it's not everything that burns.

Mutilation | Dear Eugene

> To be an ogbanje is to be categorized [as] other—and to bring alterity home in a way that transcends the more ordinary, bifurcated "otherness" of gender. This other gender is marked from birth—as male and female statuses are marked—by special behaviors towards and physical adornment of the child. The sexual appearance of the ogbanje may, indeed, be seen as a sham—yet another promise that the ogbanje is likely to break in its refusal to act according to human norms.
>
> —Misty Bastian, "Irregular Visitors: Narratives about Ogbanje (Spirit Children) in Southern Nigerian Popular Writing"

This will make sense shortly.

An ogbanje is an Igbo spirit that's born

to a human mother, a kind of trickster that dies unexpectedly only to return in the next child and do it all over again. Humans call them malevolent because, well, humans take things too personally. Ọgbanje come and go. They are never really here—if you are a thing that was born to die, you are a dead thing even while you live. Igbo ontology explains that everyone is in a cycle of reincarnation anyway: you are your ancestor, you will become an ancestor, the loop will keep looping within the lineage. Ọgbanje, however, are intruders in this cycle, unwelcome deviations. They do not come from the lineage; they come from nowhere, so it's important for an ọgbanje never to reproduce. If it did, it would contribute to the lineage, and when it died, its spirit would join those of the humans, participating in their reincarnation loop.

Removing a uterus is an efficient way to make sure this never happens.

I have always had a violent aversion toward reproduction, toward having a body that was marked by its reproductive potential—a uterus to carry children, full breasts to feed them with—it repulses me to even type this out.

Two years after I moved to Brooklyn, I had my first surgery, a breast reduction. It was an outpatient procedure: some fat removed from my chest, some glands, some skin, nothing much. It required a letter from my therapist to prove that I was sane.

"I've never heard of anyone like this," the surgeon told me. He was an old white man who had performed many surgeries on transgender patients, from breast augmentations to double mastectomies. "Male to female, female to male, fine. But this in-between thing?"

I ground my teeth into a smile and handed him the letter, along with printed images of the chest I wanted. It was one that felt right for me, one that wouldn't move much, wouldn't sway with pendulous wrongness or leave me gasping shallow breaths because my ribs were encased in the flattening black of a chest binder every day. I paid his office ten thousand dollars, skimmed from my student loans, and tried to reduce my anger at having to jump through such hoops. If I'd asked for an augmentation, it would've been fine, but wanting smaller breasts in the absence of back pain was considered ridiculous enough to require a therapist's approval. I hate humans. During my post-op visit, the surgeon complained that he'd never had to spend as much time in consultation with a patient as he had with me. We'd spent maybe thirty minutes together over a few appointments.

My scars hypertrophied, leaving shiny brown keloids and flat glossy rivers on my chest. Sometimes, back when I thought flesh terms were the only language I could use, I'd look at them to remind myself that I was "trans enough," because I'd chosen to modify my body. Even though dysphoria and surgery aren't prerequisites for being trans, the scars still served as a grounding reflection of my own certainty. I wasn't sure then what I was transitioning my body to, but I was clear that the gender I'd been raised as was inaccurate— I'd never been a woman.

After that first surgery, my depression lifted significantly. It was a connection I hadn't made before, how that physical dysphoria was affecting my mental health, eagerly contributing to my depression—I'd survived a suicide attempt just four months before the surgery. The choice to finally modify my body felt like a big deal in large part because other people treated it that way. Their alarm was almost infectious, but I was the one who had to live in this body; I was the one who suffered in it. The reduction was simply a necessary procedure, something that helped pull me away from wanting to die, something that made living a little easier.

Still, as I contemplated my second surgery, there was a deep sense of transgression about what I was doing that I couldn't shake, especially as a Nigerian. It was too easy to tune in to my community and hear the voices heavy with disgust, saying that what I had done was disfiguring, that God had made me one way for a reason and I had no right to say or do otherwise, that I was mutilating myself. There was an ideal that my body was supposed to conform to, and I was deviating from it by having surgery. I was rejecting it as a center and choosing something else: a world where the deviation itself was the ideal.

I chose it readily. I've never minded being a mutilated thing.

· · ·

THE ROBOT was called a da Vinci.

It was delicate, precise, inserted through my navel to slice my uterus and fallopian tubes into small, unimportant pieces, which were then suctioned out of my body. The procedure had a technical name that filled my mouth— a robotic-assisted subtotal hysterectomy with a bilateral salpingectomy. I had to repeat this about seven times on the day of surgery, as nurses came in with forms clarifying that I knew what I was getting, but I didn't mind. I'd waited years for this. It was the second time I was choosing to mutate my body into something that would fit my spiritself. In another life, I'd trained to be a surgeon myself, dissecting cadavers and cutting through layers of dermis and fascia and muscle with a #10 blade. But in this one I was twenty-eight and cold, my numb skin wrapped in a hospital gown as nurses draped me in warmed blankets. Still, anticipation rang clear chimes through me. I couldn't wait to be wheeled out of that operating room, finally sterile.

My best friend, Alex, flew into Upstate New York for the hysterectomy. After the excision,

they unfolded a cot in my hospital room while
I ordered waffles from room service. When
the nurses came in, they tried to get me to
stand up, but the pain was a riptide dragging me under. I swayed, nearly collapsing, so
they eased me back into bed and upped my
pain meds. I caught my breath as Alex and
I exchanged alarmed looks, their hand warm
around mine.

"I didn't think it would be this bad," I managed to say.

"Me either," they replied.

The nurse gave us a brief but incredulous
look. "You got an entire organ removed from
your body," she pointed out. "It's kind of a
major surgery."

I made it out of bed a few hours later, walking in slow motion around the hospital floor
with my IV stand rolling beside me, my palm
scraping against the walls and the nurse at my
elbow. The next day, Alex drove me home to
my attic apartment. Most of my early recovery was spent there, in a wingback recliner
the color of wet moss. It had a wooden handle
on the side that opened the back hinge and
made the foothold pop up with a creaky jerk,

stretching the chair out. I slept in it for a week because I had difficulty standing up or bending into narrow angles, and my bed was too close to the floor. I was full of stitches and hydrocodone, and my guts had been rearranged. It wasn't my first mutilation, but it was one of my best.

If ọgbanje represent an overlapping of realities—a spirit who looks incredibly convincing as a human—then what does it look like for one to experience dysphoria and take surgical steps to resolve it? It was inevitable that I'd be drawn to these overlaps, since I live there, inhabiting simultaneous realities that are usually considered mutually exclusive. What can we call the dysphoria experienced by spirits who find themselves embodied in human form? Flesh dysphoria, perhaps. Nonhuman dysphoria. Spirit dysphoria. Metaphysical dysphoria. I don't know, but it required me to modify my body to reflect the type of entity I am.

The possibility that I was an ọgbanje came to me years before I wrote **Freshwater,** around the time I began calling myself trans, but it took me a while to collide and connect the two worlds. I suppressed it for a few years because most of my education had been in the sciences and all of it was Westernized—it was difficult for me to consider an Igbo spiritual world to be equally if not more valid. The legacy of colonialism has always taught us that such a world isn't real, that it is nothing but juju and superstition. When I finally accepted its validity, I revisited what that could mean for my gender.

Do ọgbanje even have a gender to begin with? Gender is, after all, such a human thing.

In flesh terms, being trans means being any gender different from the one assigned to you at birth. Whether ọgbanje are a gender themselves or without gender didn't really matter, it still counts as a distinct category, so I didn't consider my transition to be located within human parameters at all. Rather, the surgeries were a bridge across realities, a movement from being assigned female to assigning myself as ọgbanje—a spirit customizing its vessel to reflect its nature.

It was considerably difficult to convince a doctor to remove an uninjured organ, even though my wholeness depended on its absence, especially because that organ was reproductive and they thought I was a woman. I didn't have a doctor's letter for my uterus—it was too difficult to find a therapist who had experience with nonbinary trans patients—and I didn't have money to cover the operation. But I thought perhaps I could save up for it, so I made appointments with a few gynecologists to discuss my options. I chose not to disclose my gender (or lack thereof), but instead expressed my desire for the surgery as an elective choice because I didn't want children.

The doctors received me with resistance and thin contempt. "What if you change your mind?" they asked me, in exam room after exam room, metal and glass and white coats all blurring into a single closed door. I had a thousand comebacks, but I bit them all back because these people had what I needed: gloved hands to cut me open and toss my uterus into the bright plastic of biological waste, or wherever unwanted organs end up. The dysphoria had built a tight knot of a home in my body, since I had no idea how I was going to afford another surgery or, at this rate, even find a doctor willing to perform it. It wasn't as severe as before my first surgery, but it was still there—a reminder so red it was almost black, showing up every month. I couldn't live with even a chance of getting pregnant, so I tried an IUD. When they inserted it, I screamed from the pain, the excruciating wrongness of something passing through my cervix. In the months afterward, I bled too heavily, through ultra tampons and overnight pads, flooding menstrual cups. Eventually, an ultrasound showed that the IUD was out of position, so they had to remove it. It felt like my body had spat it out, a reminder that nothing short of an excision would suffice.

By then I'd left Brooklyn and moved upstate, to the attic apartment with the moss green recliner. Occasionally, I had bouts of searing pelvic pain that trapped me in bed for hours. A few weeks into my second winter there, I went to see a urogynecologist, thinking there was something wrong with my bladder. It took the entire afternoon to run tests; then he called me into his office to tell me there was an 84 percent chance I had endometriosis. "We could put you on birth control," he suggested. I refused.

"Why not?" he asked, and just like that, the

air in his office stopped moving. I could feel
my nerves jangling, the familiar taste of the
moment right before each and every disclosure
like a sharp film over my tongue.

It's easier when I'm alone. Today, my closest family and friends are those who understand that I'm not human. Back then, I just
told them I wasn't a woman, but some continued to think of me as one anyway. I ignored
it because sometimes it's easier to not fight,
to accept the isolation of being unseen as a
safe place. Those friends fell away with time.
I exist separate from the inaccurate concept
of gender as a binary; without the stricture of
those categories, I don't have to think about
my gender, I don't even have to pretend to be
human in the first place. Alone, there's just
me, and I see myself clearly.

Speaking to other people, though, requires
channeling who or what I am into language
they can understand. It requires folding.

"I'm trans," I explained to the doctor. "And
I've had a breast reduction, so hormones would
reverse that."

He nodded while my stomach churned. "I've
had a few trans patients," he said. "We could

do a hysterectomy, if that's something you'd want. Your insurance would cover it."

I stared at him, hope and disbelief numbing my hands. I'd been terrified that he was going to say something transphobic, that I'd have to deal with the violence of that tearing through my skin, a bullet I hadn't scheduled when I showed up there that afternoon. Instead, when I left his office, I had a surgery date only two weeks away.

The robot went through my navel for the procedure, unfolding it and then tucking it back into my abdomen in a new and renovated configuration. At my post-op appointment, the doctor called the nurse over to brag about how well the wound had healed. There were only two small scars, each barely a centimeter long, at the top and bottom of my new navel.

A week or two after the surgery, I called my human mother and told her what I'd done, even though I knew she wouldn't understand. She sighed with the resignation of a mother who has tried to stop her child before and failed. "Could you **try** not to cut off any more parts of your body?" she said, and I laughed so hard my stitches hurt.

A few days later I flew to her house for Christmas, attendants pushing me around both airports in a wheelchair, weak but giddy. The rest of my recovery was uneventful. After seventeen years and approximately two hundred periods, I slipped easily into my new and bloodless life.

THERE IS a vivid history of mutilation with ọgbanje: a dead one can be cut and scarred to prevent it from returning undetected. Ọgbanje are a cohort—they separate from each other at birth, but return to the cohort when they die—and I like to think that there is a form of shared or generational memory within that. Being dead or mutilated are not unfamiliar things to any of us; we're not afraid of either.

It has been grueling to remake myself each time I learn more about who or what I am— to take the steps and bear the costs that such remaking requires. Sometimes those costs are worn on my heart, like when the people I love no longer have space in their worldview for me. Other times, it's the body that bears them, in markings and modifications. By now, I've come to think of mutilation as a shift from wrongness to alignment, and of scars as a form of adornment that celebrates this shift. The keloids on my chest and the small lines spilling out of my navel function as reminders—that even when it means stepping out of one reality to be swallowed by another, I continue choosing to move toward myself.

Execution | Dear Nonso

We've never met. This might not even be one of your many names, but I know you're out there, several people scattered across the world, storytellers who are starting out. In this letter, I think I'm teaching, sharing, because there is no unfolding of a self without the space to do it in, without the safety that my career as a writer has given me. I don't teach a lot of things, but I can try with this: the spell that I used to carry me from being a baby writer walking blind in faith and terror to where I am now, where I am sure and certain and strong in my work. This I know, as intimately as the wet side of my skin if it was taken off the muscle and held up, flapping like a sail looking for direction. The teaching helps me remember, helps me loop back into myself. Just remember that anyone can tell you their spells, but like most lessons, I don't know if it will help.

So. There are these questions about how the magic moves. Is it the rites you perform, the resources you use, or does it come from something deeper inside a person? Does the spell work for people who aren't me? I hope it does. I share it often and openly because I want it to work for others; I want it to do for them what it did for me. I think it could make so many of us safe. The magician tells me that other people can't do what I do, and maybe I believe him a little, but that's not the point. People can do such spectacular things if you forget to tell them it's impossible. I want them to **try.**

This is a spell for storytellers—for those of us who make books or are trying to. We want the work to sustain itself, we want it to feed us and keep us safe, but sometimes it feels like we're missing a map. How can we get to where we want to be? What is the hack, the strategy to make it happen? What words do you chant into the space between spaces, to bend your desires into reality?

Here's what I did. I hope it helps.

WHEN I STARTED THE SPELL, I thought about the things I wanted. After I wrote **Freshwater,** I wanted a book deal, I wanted to be able to write full time, and I wanted a Nigerian visual artist to design the book's cover. A year or two later, I wanted a bungalow, a personal hairstylist, and money. I wanted to be able to afford to keep making my work. I wanted to wear my pink faux fur to my book launch, and I wanted to stunt at awards. Right now, I want a television show and I want to be entirely out of debt. As I write this, it's the fall of 2019 and I'm lying in bed in my bungalow, planning outfits for a gala where my second book is being honored. I've been writing full time since 2014.

This is how I know that it doesn't matter if you think the goals are attainable. They are. What matters is that they are **impossible** without the work, they **cannot** happen if you don't make the work. With my spell, I drew a map of the future I wanted, then I took those defined lines and pulled them across time, dragging them into the present. Time bends very easily; you can fold it like this with little trouble. So. The spell is to make that future real, which can be done because you are not powerless, and the only thing that needs to be done in the here and now is to make the work. Or, to put it simply, all you have to do is write.

The future fans out in brilliance, powered by imagination and ego and hope and a thousand other things, but all that glory can be condensed across time into the choice to sit and write words down. It doesn't even have to be done well—that's what revision is for. It just has to be completed. There is such a space, a stretch of desert, between imagining something, writing it, and then finishing it. Execution is a particular discipline, something built out of corded rigor, tight and greased with sacrificial blood. There are many components to this spell: how to make the task at hand the only one that is real; how to work when you don't want to; how to summon your want and collar it for your purposes, setting it to work.

I bribed myself with the future. I dangled the things I wanted in front of my greedy eyes, and in the flush of that desire I reminded myself that writing five hundred words **right now** would reel in the world I wanted. There is always something you can do right now; there is always a first step, no matter how small it is. Seeds are often tiny, and it means nothing about what they will grow up to be. You plant them anyway, and that's what making the work is.

I don't think everyone believes that it can be that simple, but again, I'm not sure how making and fulfilling your own prophecies works for other people.

If you say yes with enough force, your chi will say yes, too. My chi and I are hurtling forward at breakneck speed—faster than my body can handle; my flesh breaks down at this pace. I believed in the spell with everything I had, and maybe that is the generator powering it all—that utter belief. Not on its own, but the actions that are fueled by it.

I wrote **The Death of Vivek Oji** while

Freshwater was on submission to publishers. In the fall before **Freshwater** came out, I wrote **Pet.** All you have to do is write. By the time **Pet** came out, I had completed **Little Rot.** It doesn't get easier with each one, but after the first execution, you know that the rest are possible, and with possibility you can do almost anything. You refine your spells, adjusting a touch here, a sacrifice there, but the work is a spell on its own; it does its own magic once executed.

I've watched people try to find shortcuts, hacks that avoid the work, and they end up wasting so much energy that could've been put into the work. For storytellers like us, it's hard learning how to give the work the devotion it requires, how to let the rest of the world burn, how to abandon control. It's a little like madness—and people will foam at the mouth to tell you so, as if you don't already know, as if you're not screaming inside from the fear. I don't know what to say to that. I suppose you have to be willing to go mad. Can you lose control of something you never really controlled in the first place? Illusions are the best things to burn, I think, but some people consider such fires to be threats, and those who start them even worse.

Maybe this spell is specifically for people who talk to God. I'm sure it can be adapted for others, but its foundation in God is my only point of certainty. I have no reason to believe what I believe without the flame of faith. I knew what my futures would be because they were shown to me—I don't consider myself a prophet. Obey, I was told, and receive all you desire. Again, it seems simple, but none of it is. Execution isn't, and neither is obedience; both are rife with costs, both are stained with ash from the burned offering. You get nothing for free; you pay for all of it. God asks for so much. How much will you give? Your loved ones, your reality, your friends, your pleasures, your time, your security, your sanity, your fear, your control, your illusions? How much will you **get**?

Some people can't finish the spell because they balk at the costs. That makes sense; who wouldn't? If it wasn't hard to sacrifice, it wouldn't **be** a sacrifice. This doesn't work like a crossroads deal. When I talk about the journey with my friends, we call it the desert: the place between where you came from and where you are trying to go, the hard place, a sky that drives you mad and nothing on the horizon. There is no map. There is no food and there is no water. There is manna that goes stale, there is temptation; there is God; there is a requirement for patience beyond what you thought possible, for trust beyond what seems sane; there is an end, but you cannot see it. I don't blame people for not completing the spell. It's a bloody road to stick to, simple as it is. It asks for the world and gives you silence, but part of the rigor is staying, showing up for the work regardless of the conditions. This is ritual, religion, sacrifice, magic—this is the spell.

The first time is the hardest.

It worked for me, that's all I can say. I don't know what other factors were at play, but it worked, so I stay faithful. My instructions shift, and my sacrifices do, too. I have received gifts beyond what I could have imagined for myself, and been torn apart to degrees I never thought I could survive. I think that is balance. I am also stronger than I ever thought—a beast, a god—my life is unrecognizable, and on the better days I delight in it.

I still use the spell; it is a reliable one and I want so much; I am greedy for things I never dared to want before. The spell is clear: face your work. I inhale it like a meditation sometimes, to counter the panic of a life mutating too fast, when I wake up every day as a different person inside a different world. Everything else can shift however it wants, but the work will always be the work. No matter what changes, that instruction is still the same.

What happens after you make the work might be uncertain, but one thing is guaranteed: If you **don't** make the work, **nothing** will happen. Discipline is just a series of choices. With the spell, we can understand that each choice is carving out a future, finding our way out of the desert. Trust me, it's glorious on the other side.

Deathspace | Dear Marguerite

I'm so glad I can write this letter to you—that we have formed a family built on love and choice, and that even my human mother acknowledges that I am also your child. I remember the first time I met you, at the house up the hill, when Katherine invited me to spend Christmas with her. I had been so lonely in Trinidad. I made a chocolate-and-coconut cake, put on a black dress, and smiled nervously as I said hello to you in your parlor. You were a force, gathered unto yourself, thick hair and dark eyes.

"This is my mother," Katherine said.

I'm not sure how long after that you decided to love me, but I'm glad that you did, that we've had these years with our spirits together. When I saw you last at Katherine's wedding dinner in New York, you held my face with tears in your eyes and hugged me tightly, telling me how light I had felt the time before, as if I was leaving this world. You could feel, now, that I had come back to this side, no longer teetering on the edge of death. I hadn't noticed then because I had been dying for so long. Like after **Freshwater** came out, when I thought I would die in Seattle.

We'd launched it in Brooklyn the week before, on a Tuesday night in February, at the Greenlight Bookstore on Fulton. I wish you could have been there. My first book—it should have been something unbelievably special, and maybe it was. I don't remember much of how it felt. I was sad in the car there because the magician chose not to come, chose to miss it. The store was packed wall to wall with a glorious press of gorgeous people; Yagazie flew in from wherever in the world she'd been at the time, walking around with her camera as her eye. My human mother was there, even though I'd blocked her a few weeks earlier, after she emailed me sharing her disappointment. I wasn't including my family in this happy time. I wasn't wearing the right masks, the right skins on my face. She wasn't having the experience she wanted out of this book launch. I'm supposed to reflect things, you see; they're meant to angle off me and illuminate her by proximity. It doesn't work if I don't let her close enough for the light to hit.

I OFTEN FEEL like a trophy to my parents, a shiny little prodigy who gets shamed and chastised when I step out of line—a whip of violences cracked into the air to force me back into compliance. Threaten my doctors, try to get me committed, out me, tell me I'm going to get AIDS, call me weak and a coward, tell me I'm sick in the head, then pull me close when I recoil too much, or when they're lonely, or when there is power, money, and shine on the table. Perhaps this is ungracious. I've been asked to be more empathetic, more lenient with them. In the weeks leading up to the Greenlight event, my human mother kept trying to involve me as she planned her trip, and she grew increasingly upset that I wasn't excited enough, wasn't engaging with her enough. "Do you even want me there?" she asked once, frustrated. I couldn't tell her I did, because none of my feelings matched what they should have been: they deviated from predictions, they skewed into strange places, and they exhausted me thoroughly. I could feel people's wants hammering against me, loud and hungry and scared. Big things were happening around me, flashy and powerful, the kind of things that make other people happy, but I was just quiet and sad and drowning, and so many people wanted me to reassure them that I wanted them there, that I wasn't ignoring them, that I wasn't leaving them behind, that I was still available, I was still accessible. They didn't ask how I was doing or if I was okay, but they made sharp little comments— **you don't love me anymore**—and all I could smell was their concern for their place in my new life, hands and hands and hands reaching for me. I was too tired to feel any guilt, to jump into the reactions they expected,

whatever would make them feel safe and se-
cure. So many hands, and none of them were
there to help me; none of them even **asked.** I
don't know if I've forgiven them for that, but I
don't speak to most of those people anymore,
so I guess it doesn't matter. They just wanted
to touch me, and that wasn't going to do anything other than perhaps kill me a little faster.

The months before that had already been
deadly. I should have talked to you about it;
you would've known exactly what to say. Do
you remember that afternoon when we drove
to Macqueripe with Uncle Gaby, because I
wanted to touch the water, and on the way
back he asked me what I would do if I became rich and famous? You laughed and answered for me—you told him I'd do exactly
what I was doing now—and you were right. I
loved you so much for that. All I did in those
months was write and cook in the pistachio
kitchen: ceviche from fresh red snapper, thick
homemade yogurt with local honey, cakes
and sweets and shortbreads. I am the same
under these changing faces, there's just all the
tensions between the masks as they slide on
and off.

Change is brutal, no matter how glamorous it is.

My team knew the book would be successful—we could taste it on the wind—but it didn't make me feel safe. It felt like doom, it felt like a prophecy coming true, it felt like it would be the end of me. If **Freshwater** was going to be published, if it was going to burn into the world so well, then it didn't really need me anymore. I had become redundant. This book, this thing I had turned myself inside out for, was breaking away from me and spinning up power I couldn't even imagine. I felt, very strongly, that I needed to die. It would be in service to the work: the book might sell even more attached to the story of the tragic young writer who could have had such a stellar career if their corpse hadn't been found before their first book even debuted. People would read **Freshwater** and speculate about what my career would have looked like after starting with a book this bold. I would be less of a threat, they wouldn't hesitate to call the book what it was—not the way they do when you're **alive** and young, Black and pretty and fucking talented, and you don't pretend like you don't know all of this. Some of them don't particularly want to admit that you did something this groundbreaking on your first try. All of that hesitation goes away if you're dead. Imagine a scramble for my remaining manuscripts; imagine if the best way to get this story to the people who need it was to die for it? A book about the pain of embodiment, its author killed from the very suffering the book documents? It's all deeply on brand.

I lied to my doctor that my sciatica was flaring up and I almost cried at how concerned he was, how careful, as he wrote the prescription I intended to kill myself with. Muted tangerine circles, ten milligrams of cyclobenzaprine each. They're a muscle relaxant, but I have a high sensitivity to the drug: one pill knocks me out for thirteen hours, so I was curious what an entire bottle would do. My doctor had no idea, and I wore a face so far away from death, he wouldn't have been able to guess. I just needed the pills. I needed the safety they gave—not even to kill myself with, but just to shake in my hand, to hold death there, know that it was close, comforting, like a lethal security blanket. Death has always been the thought that calms the hungry avalanche in my head. Just meditating on it lifts the weight of this world a little. I measure danger by proximity to an actual suicide attempt, how close did I flirt this time, that kind of thing. I thought that lying to get the pills was as far as I would go.

I was very fucking wrong.

After the book launch, I went home alone. I took off the pink dress I'd worn, hung up the faux fur, and washed off my makeup. I went into my kitchen and took three times as much of the cyclobenzaprine as I'd ever taken before. It was like a little suicide test run, just to see how deeply it could knock me out. Ten milligrams was my usual dose if I was in too much pain; it would steal half a day and leave me groggy for the other half. I thought perhaps thirty milligrams would knock me out thrice as deep, but instead it knocked me out for three times as long. It's interesting if you think about it, the way consciousness folds, the expectation of layers and the actuality of length. I think I slept through the next day, Wednesday, and into Thursday. I don't remember. My calendar says I had a phone interview on Thursday, but I have no idea if I made it. My family and I

had plans to go see **Black Panther.** I made it
to that, I know.

I went to the theater on Thirty-Fourth
Street, dissociating intensely, very much absent, wondering if this counted as being high.
I sat next to Yagazie and whispered to her that
I was on pills, so if I acted weird, that was
why. She nodded. We watched the movie, and
when we stood together on the street outside
afterward, my human mother tried to make
plans to see me. I was headed for the subway
station and I remember how desperate she felt
to connect with me, the way she touched my
arm, my internal recoil. She is not a safe place;
I don't trust her concern. She wants the relationship we have to match the one in her head.
I used to play along, and then I turned thirty
and stopped a little, and then the book came
out and I stopped some more, and it has just
been more and more stopping since then. I see
how that could be painful, when the masks
are put down and I shrug away from her hand
and go underground, back to my apartment,
back to the sleep that's waiting just under my
skin, to that drugged and gone place, that

you don't have to deal with how this world hurts place.

A few days later, I fly to San Francisco, and then to Seattle. Death flies with me.

I start to think about estate planning, about what to do with my unedited and unfinished manuscripts. Who should get the royalties when I die, who should be in charge of things, who will be executor of my will, who will own the literary rights—it has to be someone I trust with the stories. I text Christine from Seattle and ask her if she knows any lawyers who do estate planning. She asks me if this is part of a suicide plan. I lie and say no. She tells me that she would still help me even if it was. I know she knows I'm lying, but I don't take it back.

I feel Death pressing closer, tighter, leaning against my neck and rustling in my ear. I have so many more stops on the tour. I know I won't survive them, but it's my first book, it's the debut, it's been supported by so many indie booksellers, and I don't know how to not show up. The book is apparently doing well. The reviews are coming in and they're brilliant, I've been on the radio and written all these essays, including one published by The Cut, where I disclose that I'm trans. It's such a flesh term, but the announcement gives me a chance to talk about the dysphoria in its accurate form, as spirit at odds with flesh. I'm afraid that the true spirit affirming surgery for me might just be dying, that all these other things I do are the equivalent of binding, or tucking, or all the ways we fold the flesh we don't want, to try and get it to mimic the self we see. I want to fold the flesh right off my bones and collapse into nothing.

There is so much happening and I can't feel most of it, just Death stroking my throat and calling me home.

I call Chinelo and tell her what's happening. The rules of deathspace are that I have to tell someone, no matter how much the whispers say not to, no matter how convincing they are that all of this makes sense only in my head, that once I let it out it'll be clear that I'm lying, just looking for attention, that it's not that bad, it can't be that bad, there are people out there who actually deal with the closeness of death and this doesn't count, this is just childish nonsense, I'm not going to actually die from

it. I know by now that these whispers make
it all unreal, so that they can sever me from
this and claim me for themselves. It's how the
first attempt happened: the cops and the ambulance and the charcoal back up my throat.

So I tell Chinelo and she talks to me, re-
assures me that the first book almost takes
people out all the time, that no one talks about
it because they don't want to seem ungrateful.
She says I need to come home, come and stay
with her, so she can make sure I'm okay. It
makes me want to cry, how largely she loves me.
The magician had said the same thing, about
the debuts and the ingratitude, about how people would mock: "Oh, are your diamond shoes
too tight?" and he always wanted to tell them,
"Yes, yes, they're too tight and they're hurting
me." I imagine dancing at a literary gala wearing the diamond shoes, my feet slippery with
blood, the light catching red off the stones,
having to smile, smile, you've been reviewed in
The New York Times, in **The New Yorker,**
in **The Washington Post,** you've been in
Vogue, Annie Leibovitz shot you, aren't you
lucky, you know this doesn't happen for every
writer, even if they're brilliant like you—and

they're right. It doesn't. I'm lucky. The dance floor is streaked with me.

The hotel room in Seattle is lovely and huge and Rick Simonson, the bookseller, has sent me a saffron card, which I've saved. I'm talking at his store tomorrow, and tonight I can order whatever I want from room service because they're paying for it. I order dinner and a crème brûlée, which comes in a huge bowl, the cream poured generously in, the sugar on top scorched and crackling. I can't finish all of it, so I eat what I can and shove the rest into the minibar. The next day, the sugar crust is now just a sweet brown layer, collapsed from what it used to be. I am also collapsing.

I talk to Alex, who has had to live with the possibility of losing me for almost a decade now, and they are terrified, but they tell me how they're not the one who has to live with it, so they can't say anything, they can't really tell me to stay. I appreciate that, because so many people tell me to stay without knowing what they're asking, the kind of pain they're willing me to just continue being in, and they can't imagine that this pain has been there since I was little, since before I can remember, always and constant, and my whole life is a calculated distraction to try and get away from it. I always knew writing my books couldn't keep me alive forever, that they would run out and I'd need something else, a new treatment plan, because I'd developed a resistance to this one. The magician tells me about his father and the bus—how all you have to do is miss this bus, because another one will be coming. Another one will always be coming. You will always, at some point, want to die.

I realize I have no idea how to cancel the tour, how to stop the wheels from crushing me. I call my agent, Jackie—you'd like her—and tell her I'm dying. Not in those words, probably in more measured ones, but enough that she understands how serious it is. She's wonderful, as she always is, tells me she'll handle it with my publisher, tells me that my health is the most important thing. Jackie says that enough times in the next few months that even I start to believe it, that my well-being matters more than selling this book. That I **can** say no and stay at home, which is where I want to be, not alone in hotels, brokenhearted that the person I love is not with me, that I go out there and talk to people who love the book, love the self I wear at the readings, and that self loves them, too, but it collapses when I leave, and there is another me that belongs to just me, and it feels like that one is always sad and alone.

Jackie cancels the rest of my tour, leaving only the New York events. I tweet obscurely about it, unwilling to share the things I'm sharing now, how hard a time I'm having staying alive.

That was February. In June, I am in London, on the second little tour, when the depression hits again—a rich old white man telling people at a literary dinner I couldn't attend that I'm a liar, showing them my Instagram page to disprove my chronic pain, then emailing me to tell me about it. I sever ties with his foundation—fuck how much money they gave me—then cancel a few last things and fly to the magician, who is in a castle in Slovenia. In September, I am in Berlin on the third little tour. My human mother gives out my number without my permission. A friend accuses me of not keeping my word because she asked for money in a crisis and I had to check my budget

first. I have been taking care of her across distance this whole trip, trying to help her get
away from someone harmful. She knows how
tours almost kill me each time, but at the moment she is surviving, and that doesn't matter
to her right now. I don't matter to her right
now. I am money I won't give her immediate
access to. I am not me. The people who are
supposed to love me aren't protecting me. I am
alone. I am alone. I look at pictures of corpses
on the internet and try to hang myself from
the closet rod. There is a DO NOT DISTURB
sign on the hotel door; no one would find
me in time. My reflection is ugly, the way my
neck bulges. I abandon the tour and fly back
to Brooklyn.

I don't know what career success looks
like without all of this stitched into it—all
this pain, all this dying. I wish I was back
in Trinidad, Marguerite, watching you cook
in your chaos of a kitchen, showing you the
caramel I make from palm sugar and coconut milk, walking through the market, a different time when I was not the me that I am
now. None of this will save me—the money,
the recognition, the brilliant work, the fame.

It makes me both hypervisible and unseen. People can't imagine that I can have all the things they want and still not be okay, still be dying so fast it's incredible.

That time my human mother visited me in Trinidad was the last time I was ever alone with her. We spent twelve hours a day doing tours of the island, things she liked. I wanted her to be happy. When we finally met up with you for lunch, as soon as I stepped out of the car, you took one look at me and exclaimed, "Oh, child, you're exhausted!"

I almost burst into tears then because you could **see** me, just when I thought I had become utterly invisible. You still see me, even when I am dying. You tell me over and over again how strong I am, but in the same breath, how fragile. You hold space for the dark and brilliant things in me. Thank you, Marguerite.

In your eyes, I live a little longer.

Masks | Dear Maki

I want to take the magician who loves me back home to Nigeria. I miss the heavy air there, the way it immediately grounds you in the visceral, sinks you into a weighted reality. It's the perfect place for masquerades and tricksters, for dizzying extravagance, unapologetic performance, for corners and secrets that stare you in the eye. The magician knows a lot about masks; he's made them, spent years breathing the air seized inside them. He's also a trickster who lives in the knuckles, in the place that moves. I'm a thing of blurred spaces, too, masks slipping on and off, limited exhibitions passing through my face.

We sit in three and a half cafés at the same time and he orders us a pot of hibiscus tea while we talk about authenticity, and how stories can be more true than facts. "If you accept that masks are gateways to larger truths," the magician says, "then you can slip from the bondage of what is considered authentic. You wear the mask, you are the thing." My tea is deciding to turn into coconut water. I drink it anyway. "In possession rituals," he continues, "the god is present however the god presents, in whomever the god rides. The god cannot be inauthentic."

I know from my childhood, between Aba and Umuahia, that it is the same with masquerades: if you wear the costume, you are the spirit. We used to watch them from the window of my father's car, spirits running along the roadside, collecting payments from the drivers. Looking at a masquerade isn't free, even if you think it is—especially if you take a picture. I wonder what they could look like in a different world—drenched in blue, perhaps, like the Paramin devils in Trinidad. Or a surveillance of plastic faces, blood-red arms waiting in a row of corn.

I haven't worn a solid mask in a long time, except for one the magician gave me before a flight to Bulgaria. I took a picture of myself in it when I got to Singapore and sent him the image. It was the kind of mask you could fold up and cram into an insignificant space, which was useful; I don't have room in my suitcase for anything harder. Besides, I've got roughly sixty-seven other masks, and all of them live in my face.

They used to be strictly instruments of concealment for me; I thought I had to strip them away, turn myself into a thing with an open throat and a plucked body, peel back broken plastic to show the blessed object beneath. In a search for what was real, I was viewing the masks as untrue, falsehoods layered on top of whoever I was. If I committed to this excavation, I thought, I could distill myself down to some sort of fundamental core.

The tea leaves in the strainer spill across the table, spelling out letters in graffiti. The magician wipes it with a napkin, and they dry on the white cloth as printed blue font. Around us, doors in two different cafés open and close simultaneously, amputating the voices of strangers into half-formed syllables.

If you release the idea of an essential self, throw it naked into the surf and let the sea carry it away, then everything changes. Without it, masks take on a new expanse of possibility. They can conceal, yes, but as the magician says, they can also clarify what is true—in precisely the same way a story can tell you something better than stark facts ever could. They can hold you together like a tight cellophane bandage over curved metal, like a gaze across two bodies, a starched knot whorled in gold. They can be adornment, clothes as costumes that mask the body, bright enough to direct your eyes.

We are what we choose to do, which can be as simple as which mask you pick. You wear the mask, you are the thing. For people who live in the knuckles with sixty-seven faces, it's not really about pretending to be people you're not. It's more about having faces for all the things you already are—blurred spaces, trickster mobility. In the space of teatime, one of the cafés we're sitting in has been demolished. The other two and a half have dimmed their lights. The teapot curls up and falls asleep as leafy vines crawl up the table legs. All of the floors are pale sand. I hold the magician's hand and his copper fingertips break off into my palm. "A present," he says, "for later." A colorful cloud of slashed tulle falls from the ceilings.

A mask doesn't always look the way you think it does. It can be a total smear of pigment, a stamp made of sand, or sometimes—like a lot of ours—it can look like nothing at all. But it can still make you into whatever you create: the inhuman face in the forest at night, a figure resplendent on the shore, a haloed soul floating on the water. All these things are as true as you want them to be.

The magician's tea has turned into the ocean. He drinks it anyway.

Propagation | Dear Katherine

There are three varieties of the pothos vine in my apartment. The golden pothos is green, splashed with a mild yellow variegation, like dappled sunlight came to live in the leaves. My human mother has several of these in her house. She sends me a video that traces one of the vines along her walls, trying to connect over the few things we have in common: a need to grow winding plants, an attachment to the evidence that we've stayed somewhere long enough to warrant a vine doubling, tripling, in length. I ignore the video; there are more wounds between us than longing and lonely stems can knit closed.

I bought my neon pothos from a website. It was so delicate when it arrived, I felt like it hadn't been a plant for very long. The bright lime leaves were too soft, their stems too thin. I worried about it and kept it on the sill of my bedroom window, watering it more than the others, wanting it to get bigger, stronger. It spent its first week with me wilting like my heart.

The marble queen pothos was an impulse buy from a grocery store on Sixth Avenue. It was so full, spilling out of its pot, and I wanted my life to feel that full. I still want my life to feel that full.

There is a cord I have that's the same color as my neon pothos. It charges my portable speaker when it works, but right now it doesn't work; it's tied into a slipknot and shoved into the bottom drawer of an expensive dresser I bought in Soho when I came into money this year. There is a video on my phone that shows the neon wire knotted to one end of a pink flowered scarf, a lime-green noose. The other end of the scarf is tied to a thick metal rod stretching across the wood of a wardrobe in my Berlin hotel room. My pothos is too weak to do anything, but this cord is a better vine; it holds my neck when I kneel inside it, pressing against my carotid artery. (This part is not in the video.) I am investigating how to hang yourself by partial suspension. An online forum offers specific instructions, including pictures of successful corpses. The hotel mirror catches my reflection, flesh swollen under my jaw, and revulsion cuts me. I slide out of the noose and crawl to the bathroom floor, curling up like a dying shoot, hyperventilating into the tile. A few hours later, I cancel the rest of my tour and fly back to my apartment. I have been away for a week. In that time, three of my thirty plants have died, but all the pothos vines, even the sickly lime one, are alive. Almost, but not quite, like me. Two of them have new leaves.

It is possible to propagate a pothos vine from a cutting. It's easy, in fact, as long as you preserve a node; just place it in water and it will grow roots. You can keep it there if you like, watch the roots grow and tangle like confused loss, like hope, like they're searching for solid ground. It won't die. It won't rot. It will spill in two directions, insistently alive despite the amputation, glorious with its wounds. It's not easy to kill a pothos; that's why some give its name over to the devil.

It's not easy to kill me either. I am, at once, the person most bent on my death and the person most successful at keeping me alive; even the devil won't take me. After Berlin, I decide to propagate a vine of myself, to trace a node that has a chance at being happy, sever the stem beneath it and plunge it into water that perhaps understands what being loved feels like. It seems important to start over, to graft varieties onto myself: a jade arm, golden eyes, speckled silver legs, a marble queen throat. To move like the vine does—slow and languid, but determined, made of photosynthesis and direction instead of pickled pain.

The slipknot is still in the drawer. When my speaker runs out of battery, I will need to untie it. The neon pothos is doing better; a few leaves have turned brown and I've plucked them off, but the rest seem sturdy. It drinks in the late-afternoon light; a bright leaf curls over the lip of its terra-cotta pot. I suspend the golden pothos from a corner of my living-room ceiling, by a steel hook and a golden chain. When the vine gets long enough, I will direct it over my walls and windows, evidence that I stayed alive long enough for something.

I take a cutting of the marble queen pothos, three leaves and a branched stem, and put it in a glass jar of water on my desk. I'm waiting for it to grow roots, small wriggling white things that don't need the ground. I make sure the sunshine bleeding through my window brushes against the glass. The wound on the first plant will close over, like wounds should.

I wait for mine to catch up.

Canon | Dear Daniel

My childhood can be measured easily, in pools of light spilling onto pages and books blanketing the surfaces of our house in Aba. When the electricity died, as it often did, I read by candlelight or with a torchlight balanced against my body. Both my parents had been heavy readers; they dragged their libraries into their marriage and kept them separate, distinct, as if they both knew their relationship would end. My father had a collection of Reader's Digest condensed novels on the top shelf of the bookcase in my brother's room. In one of them, a little boy called his sister stupid because she was seven years old. I took it personally when I first read it, bristling with rage, because I was seven, too. That didn't mean we were stupid.

When my parents discovered I'd started reading the sex-advice columns in my mother's magazines as a child because I had run out of material, they quickly bought me more books. Stories became my entire world, unchecked and unrestricted; I was nine when I read V. C. Andrews's **Flowers in the Attic,** which I think is entirely too young for a child as lonely as I was. My sister and I rummaged through my mother's trunk, a steel tomb tucked in a corner of the house, and we found a copy of Daphne du Maurier's **Rebecca,** with that haunting first line: "Last night I dreamt I went to Manderley again." My father's library had a copy of Ken Follett's book **The Key to Rebecca,** which I'd read before, and eleven-year-old me was in awe at finding a book that I'd first read about inside another book; worlds eating worlds, all made by words.

By the time I started college in the States, I'd read every book in my childhood home.

The white dean of my school kept introducing me as the sixteen-year-old freshman from West Africa who'd already read Dickens and Tolstoy and Dostoevsky, as if any of that was surprising or special. I'd only read those books because they were there; the awe associated with a certain European literary canon wasn't relevant. I'd also read Cyprian Ekwensi, Ayi Kwei Armah, Buchi Emecheta, Chinua Achebe, the secret copy of **The Joy of Sex** hidden away in my parents' room, every encyclopedia entry in my school library on Greek mythology, labels on shampoo bottles, the sides of cornflakes boxes and Bournvita tins during breakfast, countless contraband Harlequin and Mills & Boon romance novels bartered with secondary-school classmates, narrative interludes in my brother's video games, and all the parts of the Bible that referenced sex. It wasn't until much later that I realized that there was a canon I was expected to prioritize, especially if I wanted to consider myself a writer, that the work of dead white men could be a type of currency.

A few years ago, during a nonfiction workshop at my MFA program, I read Vladimir

Nabokov for the first time. The workshop was mostly white, except for me and two other writers of color, and we'd been assigned his memoir, **Speak, Memory.** I hadn't expected much before reading the book, but I ended up delightfully surprised at how strongly it resonated: the ways in which Nabokov engaged with his own selfhood, the thinking that unspooled from that, how it reflected what I was doing in the debut novel I was working on. I felt like I'd found a precedent for what I was creating.

On the day of the workshop, we were all asked to bring in pieces we'd written, to be critiqued after we discussed the assigned reading. I brought the requested printout of my work, as did all the white writers, but the other two writers of color had nothing to turn in.

"It's Nabokov," they said. "No one writes like he does. No one can do what he does." They were so intimidated by his brilliance that they'd chosen not to present their own writing. I didn't know how to respond, but my enthusiasm about the connection I'd felt with his work dimmed into a guarded wariness. In the air of that room, as everyone agreed with them about how untouchable Nabokov was, it felt as if the only permitted emotion was awe, like anything else would be seen as incredibly arrogant. I wasn't supposed to read Nabokov and think, "Ah, we're doing something similar with this study of the self." I was supposed to be intimidated, worshipful. I was off script.

In the moment, I figured they knew better. They'd read more than I had; I was clumsy and naive to see a potential peer in Nabokov. As a young writer working on their first book, it made me even more nervous about what I was writing, the ways my work deviated from other stories that were out there. I was besieged with anxieties: What if I wasn't allowed to do what I was doing? What if it didn't get published? What if the gatekeepers read it and saw it as arrogant, me stepping out of place, writing about metaphysical selves as if I had the creative freedom of a white writer in this industry? I knew the world saw me as a Black writer, as an African woman even though I wasn't a woman, and I'd read enough about racism in publishing to worry about how it would play out in real time against me.

I kept looking for stories like the one I was

telling, but I couldn't find them, and that terrified me. Maybe I was meant to be writing stories that looked more like what popular African writers had done before; maybe if I stuck to themes that were familiar, perhaps even expected, I could have some of the success they had. I couldn't blame the other writers of color in my workshop for swallowing their work instead of presenting it. They were hearing the same message, broadcast by the limited range of our stories made available to us, a message that seemed to tell us which of these stories would be allowed through the gates and which would be held back. "When you read work like Nabokov's," the message said, "turn your face away. That's not the kind of work you can make. There's a script for people like you; stick to it."

I've been a reader all my life; I know books can be many things. My favorites are the ones that function as portals into other constructed worlds. I've loved those since I was a child; it's why I read so much speculative fiction. Some books are windows into another's experiences, or even into our own—demonstrating our raging desires to be seen and to see ourselves—but

I wonder if it is enough, this reflection of known things.

As I clawed my way through my manuscript, I remained deeply doubtful about its future. When it went out on submission, none of the rejections surprised me. I'd prepared myself for them—not because of the writing, per se, but because of the market. The book wasn't "immigrant experience" enough; it was too internal; wouldn't it be difficult to sell a book so deeply rooted in Igbo ontology to a U.S. audience? I occasionally talk about placelessness as it attaches to myself and my life, but in my fog of worry, that feeling seemed to extend to my book, wrapping it in blurry tentacles.

Months later, after it finally sold, I was composing a description of it with my editor and agent when the word "identity" came up.

"We can't use that word as is," I wrote in an email. "Everyone's going to assume that we mean national or racial identity, just because I'm a Nigerian writer. We have to specify that it's about metaphysical identity."

"Are you sure you want to use the word 'metaphysical'?" they asked.

"I know it might sound pretentious, but I

honestly don't know another accurate word," I wrote back.

My main character's life and experiences weren't centered on her being African, or Black, or an immigrant. Those were negligible, secondary. Her core conflict was that she was embodied: that she existed, that she had selves, that she was several. I didn't know any other books by African writers that asked or answered the questions I was working with, but I very much wanted to find precedent. I figured that would tell me if what I was doing was permissible or possible, that it would allow me to predict the trajectory of the book and afford me some security. Sometimes we don't get the reassurances we want; we make the work anyway. By then, I knew what it was like to look for books that reflected my world and not be able to find them. I know the power of people feeling seen, having access to stories that mirror their own, and what that experience can move inside them.

I wonder if it's enough. I know, for me, it's not.

. . . .

IT IS SUMMER in New York and I am at a cathedral uptown, meeting with Katherine Agyemaa Agard, a Trinidadian writer whose work and mind I love. We walk past the ceiling that looks like nothingness and climb into the ornate choir section. I give her a signed advance copy of **Freshwater** and she gives me a spray of velvet orange flowers. We eat two tangerines, piling the rinds sweetly around us. Katherine is telling me about her book **Of Colour** and its strangeness, how she's not sure it is actually a book; we are thinking about what a book can be. I tell her how I want reflections that are alive, that shift things for me instead of showing me the familiar. Perhaps it's because I couldn't find my own world when I looked for it in books, and though I found other worlds there—ones I've lived in, pretended in, moved through—it has never felt like enough.

So instead I turned to work that didn't reflect my story, but made me want to write new ones. I fell for books that challenged form and convention because something in them challenged me. Within the cathedral's quiet, I tell Katherine about Alain Mabanckou's **Broken Glass,** punctuated with commas alone, and

Helen Oyeyemi's **Mr. Fox,** storytelling within storytelling, blurred realities. I use my phone to pull up the ebook of Fran Ross's 1974 novel, **Oreo,** and show her the first two pages, with the diagrams and the equations, the magnificent things Ross did with structure. "**That's** an alive reflection," I say. "It's the kind of work you'd think only white writers get to make."

Katherine picks up what I'm saying about inert reflections. "They're not reformulating anything," she says. "They're transporting between ideas that already exist. Nothing is being shaped from the unknown into . . . well, something that is still unknown, really. Alive reflections are writing into the unknown."

I imagine this kind of writing as casting out into unformed space, tracing blindly, discovering something through the writing of it. I'd started my book because I had a slew of questions about existence that I was trying to figure out, rooting the process in Igbo reality and my own archive, excavating my own self, but I'd continued with it because it was also a reflection for those of us living in shifting realities, worlds framed as madness, bordered by unknowns. To write into that space was the only way I knew how to confront it, how to start wrangling a semblance of peace through the storm I'd been hiding in my head, and nothing has surprised me more than having the resulting book be read and received well. It allows me a wary hope that space will be made for writers of color working in the experimental, that we'll get to see more and more of our own books, showing us we can tell all kinds of stories and write whatever reflections we want. We don't have to swallow our work or be afraid that it's too deviant to do well, we don't have to worry about sounding pretentious or not measuring up to dead white men because there is, in fact, no canon we cannot touch. Even when seized by a thousand fears, we can make strange and wonderful things simply for the sake of the strange and the wonderful, we can create without permission, we can write into the unknown.

Deity | Dear Eloghosa

I need to tell you about a turning point.

I used to spend a lot of time trying to figure out why I couldn't detach from this world, float the way other nonhumans like you and Ann do. I studied Rumi for months—making notations, copying out quotes by hand as if they could travel up my fingers, pierce my skin, take up home in my flesh. **When craving comes, then virtue is concealed; a hundred veils divide the heart and sight.** I thought if I could unshackle myself from the flesh, from the desires of this world, I would be free, and the pain would stop. But that's a lie; even Rumi said it wasn't true. **The pain that the Creator wills is useful.** Still, there was something there, something of spirit, something I wasn't getting right. I had touched it before; I remember explaining it to the monk in Bulgaria with the stained-glass eyes. I remember how he stared at me. "People spend years in the monastery trying to get to what you just said," he told me. Rumi had said, **God's shadow is the servant of the Lord; he's dead to this world and alive to God.** How do you die without killing your body? **Each moment you have death and the return—the Prophet said the world is for an hour.** It's like Shams said. **There is only one way to be born into a new life—to die before death.** Or the Drowned God. **That which is dead may never die.**

I've written before about being an ọgbanje, that if you are born to die, then you are a dead thing even while you live. I learned so much from being a dead thing, unseen even when in bare sight, nowhere no matter where I go. Every time I made a new home, all my parlors were graves, all my roofs were earth. I became a void and it was earbleed loud, but I was dead and happy and just starting. I put my teeth in the back of fear's neck and shook it till it was limp, till it surrendered. I catloped after happiness, tackled it down, and dragged it home by the bloody throat. Who dares tell me I can't have everything? My God, I'm coming over the hill, I'm a monster. I tried not to forget it. You reminded me often; thank you so much for that.

I have a note—something you told me once when we were talking about humans. "They will serve," you said. "They are dealing with a god at all times, even when you don't remember your own self."

You were right, I didn't remember—not because it wasn't true, but because it wasn't true all the time. If a mask is also a face, a collection of sixty-seven masks is a collection of sixty-seven faces. I'm still counting them, trying to throw away the ones that are made of poor human skin, empty-eyed rotted things, puppets. I made the ogbanje face when I carved my cheeks in St. Augustine as the new year exploded; that one is comfortable, but old now. The face of a dead thing, the void—the Baron's childwife, really, fuck me in a fresh grave—while that face is true, it wouldn't stay all the time. So, I thought I was failing.

You and I talked about compassion often, about grace, about trying to be more like God. I started to think of it as attaining some sort of enlightened status, leveling up as a nonhuman entity, moving from superficial fleshlike things toward a state of deep spirit. Rumi was all about that shit: destroying the ego, killing want and attachment. **I do not chant this spell out of desire,** he wrote, **for I have turned desire upon its head. And God forbid I want something from others. There is a world of peace within my heart.** I couldn't forgive myself. The magician would say that's so Catholic of me. Why did I keep wanting so goddamn much? Why couldn't I find peace? I prayed every night. **There is a drop of knowledge in my soul. Free it from lust and from the body's earth!**

Last year, I flew to LA to spend Christmas with Ann. We sat in my hotel room for hours, night crawling into early morning, pulling at threads in questions, following the whorls that unspooled from it. What roads could we build to sustain these embodiments? How were our experiences alike? How were they different? What exactly did deep spirit mean? I'd been viewing it as a state both humans and non-humans could access, where Rumi lived. **One drowned beyond all hope of being found, and none would know him now except the ocean.** Ann is centered in deep spirit; she has the opposite problem I have. She can't seem to stay in her body, I can't get out of mine.

One thing I know about myself, though, is that I always fumble when I start thinking there's something "extra" I have to do to live as a spirit. Like in Trinidad, before I marked my face, when I kept thinking of spirit and human as a binary, either one or the other, even though the whole point of an ọgbanje is that it's both. An ọgbanje is only an ọgbanje when it is in a human body. It's not a spirit possessing a human; there is no demarcation between the two—there is no two in the first place. I didn't need to **do** anything to move as an ọgbanje. I was already doing it, by existing, by breathing. There's something in here about the misguided way people search for authenticity.

The other piece of this map is my correct

name: the deity's child, Ala's somethingborn. If my mother is a python, then so am I; if my mother is a god, then so am I. That's how it finally clicked—I can't reach deep spirit because I'm a particular kind of spirit, an embodied one. Not just an ọgbanje but an embodied god, and that's **specific.** Embodied gods are not above fleshly things, they revel in them. They wield the flesh wildly, and the consequences are not the same. No one knows if humans take it as far as gods or gods take it as far as humans, who was made in whose image, that's not the point. The point is: even if I hold the voidface, the dead thing, I'm still hyperpresent in the flesh. The flesh can be dead if it likes, but the god who animates it will always be louder.

Ann shook her head at me when I told her all this. "That's what I've been **saying,**" she laughed, with that delicious little gap in her front teeth. "Even years ago, before we started talking, I'd say, 'Akwaeke is a god! Why are they moving like that?'"

She was right: once I realized I was a small deity, I had to move differently. If my whole mother is the Ala of Odinaala, of Omenala, the one who is everywhere, a shrine in every compound? Ah-ahn. It's enough. Birthright loops a quick knot around doubt and strangles it. I can't move afraid when I'm a god. In this flesh world? The fear doesn't make sense. I can do what I want—who can touch me? A human can't enact consequences against things like us, we're not even moving in the same dimensions.

Back when I was studying Rumi, I tried reaching for humility, a sort of grace, rising above things, deep wells of compassion and all that shit. I'm not saying there aren't gods like that; I'm just saying I'm not one of them. Maybe it's also an ọgbanje thing; my brothersisters are terrible little spirit children, you know? I think they gave me some trickster residue—not the actual trickery, but the unrepentant part has to come with that kind of mischief, the petty and vindictive. Quick to burn things down. If you take traits like impatience and a hot temper, and plug them into a god already annoyed at being put into flesh, you end up with a nature I can't believe I spent so much energy trying to repent from. What god doesn't come with a streak of brutal?

But it's fine, I'm still mostly sweet, I think. This is just one of the faces—the bratty deity.

If we allow our respective birthrights, how else can we move but as mad and arrogant gods? Rightness sits strong in your bones when your parent is divine. Between you and me, our temperings are different—siblings are never the same—but we've both been taught fear, conditioned by the humans. They had their reasons, but you can't keep things like us folded for too long, the creases can't hold. I know you've felt the seams bursting, too, how much it hurts, how terrifying it is because we know how terrifying we are, they must have folded us for a reason, we're going to hurt the humans if we expand fully, we're going to burn everyone we care about, we burn too bright, it's not safe to exist, we're dangerous, we're dangerous, we're **dangerous**!

The only right thing to do is cage ourselves, wrap the collar around our throats and pull it tight, lash our own backs, save them all from us. How many times have we tried to stand up fully only for them to tell us that we're being violent for just trying to be whole, that our attempted wholeness was hurting them? They've lied to us for such a long time. And I think when we've been taught to be afraid of ourselves in such ways, we absorb some of our teachers' fear. I wonder what terrified them about us, like I kind of want to know the fine details. Is it that our spirits were too large to control? Had they just never seen anything like us before? I'm so glad we found each other at the end of the day; being witness to you is one of the joys of my life, I swear.

My therapist told me that when people think about power, they think about the choices that power will give them: options, resources, things like that. What they don't often think about are the consequences of power. The things you lose, the things you sacrifice, the costs. It was great hearing that, because of course I knew about the costs but it makes such a difference to hear them framed as a direct consequence of power. No one has patience for hearing about the consequences unless they're experiencing them as well; otherwise, all they can see are the choices. As in, life must be sweet where

you are! That's one of the more insidious ways
this kind of power just isolates you from other
people: it's like they become blind to what's
actually happening with you, replacing it with
an illusion they created, their imagination of
what your life is like, which is really a fantasy
of how they think their life would be if they
had what you have. The magician explained
this to me. You and I know it well, it's why
we're taking our time to become the beasts we
are. Consequences are things we're learning to
handle in small doses.

Like that thing where you show someone
just a little bit and they run, and then you
think, wow, if just this terrified you—the tip
of a feather—how am I supposed to open up
entire wings? If I'm already so alone with this
useless human face pressed over mine to make
you more comfortable, how bad will it get if
I show you my nonhuman faces? Ann worries
about this, too, all the time, because the hurt
the humans feel will pierce its way through
her as well. I hate that pain. I spent the other
day sobbing for hours on my bathroom floor,
because my human mother will never see me
and all she knows is that the child she bore

does not want to be close to her, and I can feel her hurt and she doesn't think I know, but of course I know, it just changes nothing, the woman suffers for being a deity's surrogate. There is no lonely like a god's lonely; I suffer in different directions.

We should just become utter and complete beasts, anyway, fuck it all.

These humans are so loud in how they press down, in how they enforce their realities. What would it look like if we took up our own space, **all** of our space, planets and planets worth of it? They won't like it, I know, but Elo, how long can we stay dungeoned just because they're afraid of us? Let them look at us, let their eyes bleed, they don't see us anyway. It's actually impressive, how someone can work so hard to crush a thing they can't see. Maybe they use their other senses, maybe they can smell things more powerful than them, feel the danger in the small hairs of their necks. I do think we're dangerous, just not in the way they told us we were. In this their world, it's dangerous to not be afraid. Do you know what kinds of things we can do without fear? You can't control a thing that doesn't understand fear, you can't condition a thing that doesn't experience consequences.

Did you ever watch the Alexander McQueen documentary? There's a quote that Jahra pulled from it and shared: **I didn't care about what people thought of me and I didn't care what I thought of myself.** Okay, we've heard the first part before, but fuck, that second part? To not care what you think of yourself? You and I talk often about making unleashed work— like what you've done with **Vagabonds!**— about writing without any censorship, writing the way we think, not translating it for the humans or the West or the white people, not worrying if it fits form, if it has precedent, if we'll be able to make a living from it, just writing because these stories, these words, are the truest things we know. And McQueen was here talking about removing not just the collar other people put on him, but, more important, the collar he put on himself! It blows my mind—to free yourself from yourself, to hear the voice in your head saying all the things it's been conditioned to say, and then to ignore it and make the work anyway? I love this idea so much—especially because it doesn't demand that you **not** think things of yourself. You can think whatever you want, just don't care about it. That's wild. That's some next-level magic.

We've spent too long with the leash of what other people think on us. We mask so well for them; we know how to see through their eyes, how to climb in and lean against their retinas. When I look at myself through them, I know to fold this part, turn down the volume here, accentuate there, so I can pass, so they can think they see me and that creates a gentleness there. They can't actually see me, but they need to **think** they can. We justify needing them to buy into the illusion, the glamour we spin so prettily for them, because that gentleness they have evaporates the moment you show yourself to be a loud, illegible thing. Now you've become unknown, now you're a threat, a thing to be brought down, torn into pieces they can chew and swallow, you know?

But the thing is, they don't **see** us. So, in using their eyes, not only do we unsee ourselves, but we also stop existing even for ourselves, which is such a cruel thing. What kind of looped violence? Fuck their eyes, may they bleed out of their heads. We deserve so much better, my love. I hope we find it all, and more.

I can't wait to see what you turn into.

Training | Dear June

imagine I am writing this to whoever you will end up being three lifetimes later, when the door slips and you remember a time when a god made you her surrogate and you had to watch your second child nearly die more times than they ever told you. We're not going to meet after this round, I know that much. This is my last one, if I have anything to do with it, and you have a few more reincarnations left to go. In one of them, you will be able to face true things without running, without striking out your own eyes. Maybe then this letter will be clear; maybe a lot of things will be clear then. Maybe you won't remember any of it.

In this lifetime, however, you were assigned as my human mother. I often describe you as an excellent guardian—a deliberate detachment, for reasons I am tired of talking about. I have multiple mothers, a fact that you ignore or accept, depending on how you feel, a depth of water I have stopped trying to fathom. I think about how difficult it would have been for me to be alive if you had not been assigned to me—but that fork in the road is a different self, a different set of genes, a different reality. For embodied nonhumans, existence is more difficult than I can ever put into words, no matter how many books I write. It makes no sense on a fundamental level, let alone when you add the other layers: navigating a human society, the institutions, the paperwork, the unyielding bureaucracy. There are two things I would like to thank you for.

The first is for training me. You have always been a beast at moving through this world, learning and adapting with a gritted tenacity. I ask myself often how quickly I would have died if I had stayed at home, if the land would have yawned open and eaten me up, reuniting me with the other side. I was already slicing my flesh open at twelve, showing off my blood to my classmates, the smile of my skin. It continued for thirteen years. You knew about it and never said anything. I know many people survive, but I also think people glorify resilience a little too much, forgetting that the fragile ones simply die as the world walks on over their bones. There are some things we shouldn't be boasting about.

When you said you were going to Baltimore to meet our immigration lawyer, I was excited because it was your first time meeting him in person after ten years of working together. You frowned when I told you this. "It hasn't been ten years," you said. "It's been twenty." That blew my mind, because it meant you'd been planning this for a whole decade before you even started executing it—how to extract us and bring us somewhere else with you, give us green cards leading to different passports, change the way we could move across borders. You were planning it when you took us to Malaysia and taught us how to navigate airports, what the signs meant, in preparation for when we would have to travel without you. In another reality, I would never have left the confines of my human father's imagination, which had retracted inward, a tight radius around where he was born and raised. Left to him, he would have kept us at home, entombed with him.

The second thing I want to thank you for is for leaving him. There is so much I wouldn't have known was possible if you hadn't done it first: to leave a husband, make a life for yourself in new countries and cities, buy a house in a place that was not home, learn a system through its violences well enough to make a bruised space for yourself within it. I remember the trips you made down from Saudi to train me for the SATs, because everything was a system that could be learned, money and luck would make up the difference. When I started my freshman year in college, we opened bank accounts in my name and a credit card to start building my credit. I was sixteen.

This system is not made for us, though, and despite the ways I tried to hack my way through it, it nearly killed me. So I have learned and I have unlearned, and somewhere in the middle

of all that is a balance, a dance between falling
blades and sheets of fire, how to use a sword
that cuts into your palm to hack open a space
in a bleeding forest. There is still no winning.
I use my training to get through graduate
schools, to get my paychecks before I drop out,
to escape hospitals that want to lock me up. I
perform and pretend, a violent farce that keeps
me alive. I know how to find apartments and
furniture, how to buy cars, how to file taxes,
how to avoid overdraft fees—a thousand little
tasks that are so fucking hard if no one trains
you, even more so if no one trains you **and** you
are an embodied spirit who wants to die.

So many people are terrified of leaving, of
having to start all over again, and other cruel
people use this as a leash. It's incredibly hard
to walk away, step into something you can't
see, but I watched you do it all my life, even
when it meant leaving me behind, eight years
old and sobbing behind lace curtains. You left
your families and communities more times
than I know to make something new somewhere else: London, Umuahia, Aba, Riyadh,
Jeddah, Ta'if, Albuquerque. Ten years in each
country and then all over again. I have never

thought of you as saving me, but I know that, because of your training and example, I know how to save myself—even, or especially, from you.

I know how to walk away and start all over again, no matter who I leave behind: a father, a husband, a brother. I have spent so long trying to unfurl myself; how could I stay where I was required to fold, where I was flattened by force, a man's hand with velocity behind it, a wicked word, lies upon lies upon lies. I could have left you behind as well, even with everything you've done for me, because I can't forget the wounds that came from your hands. The magician asked me once, over a small table in Chinatown, if I would ever forgive you. I said no, but I don't think he understood that I'm not interested in punishing you either. That all I've wanted is to not be harmed by people claiming to love me, to not have to protect myself constantly from them. That I allow you because you trained me.

So, here we are: the surrogate and the deity's child. Like I said, I don't think we'll meet again, if this is my last life. I've decided to take care of you while avoiding your dangerous proximity, your lonely and greedy version of love. This distance is just honest; perhaps in three lifetimes you'll see how the true space between us was an endless cavern, a rift that none of your longing could ever pull closed. It wasn't personal, though it certainly feels that way now. I know you don't like it, but I don't know what else to tell you. I'm not the one who arranged this. Take it up with the gods.

Worldbending | Dear Kathleen

Sometimes, you remember me better than I remember myself.

I think that's important in a friendship—to hold reflections of people for them, be a mirror when they start fading in their own eyes. I hope I do the same thing for you, too. I can't wait for you to get here for Christmas; I know Germany has been hard on you this fall.

The last time we texted, you wrote, **I need you and our time this break.** I know what you mean. The world can be a grit that sands away at us, and love can be a shelter from that. If this godhouse in the swamp is a wing, then I imagine you arriving and joining me underneath it, where we make syrup with the chocolate habaneros from my garden and sit out on the haint-blue porch. I wish the house was bigger, five or seven bedrooms instead of three, so I could fit more of us in here. We are safer with each other. We see the worlds we're trying to make, and we lend our power to each other's spells. I was steaming baos in my kitchen today and I got so excited to show you this house, my house. Just a year ago, you came down to the swamp for Christmas and we stayed in that sublet and cooked fish fresh from the lake. And now I have this house, this land, and the shock of what I made happen still makes me reel when I look at it fully. You think I'd be used to it by now, the way I can make things come true, but every year it expands. Every year I make bigger and bigger things happen—and it's not just me, obviously. It's my chi and the deityparents and God and so on, but I have to say yes first and I have to do the work and I can't believe it works.

You know how people are so in awe of Octavia Butler's journal, the way she wrote down what she wanted with her books? I think it's because written worldbending resonates so widely. I've been curious about what other languages one can worldbend in, though, languages of manifestation, if you like. Writing things down, using images to make vision boards, speaking things aloud—these are all spells. Most of my own worldbending is very action-based: I move as if the future I want is absolutely assured, making choices and spending money like a prophet—buying clothes for galas before I was ever invited to one, paintings for a bungalow I had no idea how I'd ever afford, the pink faux fur for my book launch before I even had a book deal, shit like that. And see, this is why I love you, because you never thought it was impossible; you dream even bigger for me than I do for myself. I ran the potential outfits for make-believe events by you and you took them all seriously. When the noise started happening for my book, I told you I was shocked, and you immediately called me a liar. "You said this would happen," you reminded me. "You're not surprised! Don't act surprised."

Man, I'm **supposed** to act surprised, though.

We all know the thing of how Black artists are meant to be grateful and humble, but when I started entering literary circles as a baby writer, there was all this culture I knew nothing about. That MFA program I was in, when you came to help me after my surgery, it was full of writers who were afraid. I don't mean that in a bad way; there's nothing wrong with fear. I just wasn't afraid of the same things. I wasn't worried about failing, because if I failed my life would be just the same as it already was, so there was nothing to be scared of. If I succeeded, however, everything would change, and **that** was terrifying.

I call this a culture because that's what it was. I've seen it in several places: people bonding over insecurities and self-deprecation, constantly saying they didn't think their work was good, looking to the faculty for validation, someone to tell them they were real writers, to give them direction and guidance and a map to where they wanted to go. Institutions love that, I think. It makes you need them. And all those feelings are valid, but the resentment and hostility when you don't play along, when you don't shit on your own work, when you don't wear doubt like a blanket around your shoulders? That's the part I have a problem with. It reminds me of that thing back home where people want you to "humble yourself" and sometimes their demand is quiet, sometimes it's blatant, but either way, they make sure you feel it.

I remember the dinner where I told my cohort that I'd finished my manuscript for **Freshwater,** the awkwardness that followed, their lack of excitement for me even though this was the thing we were all here for, all supposed to be helping each other toward. I went to the bathroom and one of them, a white girl, started talking shit about me as soon as I was away from the table. Later, when I announced a paid summer residency, she made a Facebook post mocking my accomplishment. When I signed with my agents, only the two Black students in the school congratulated me. No one else even acknowledged it—and my cohort eventually shut me out, even though there were only six of us. Our movie plans evaporated; the five of them got lunch together and never invited me again. I had spent my first year there trying so hard to be in community; I'd made

flans and shown up to the potlucks and believed everything they'd told me. It hurt to be
cut out—but on the other hand I was grateful
for the silence because it had been exhausting
trying to figure out how to fit into their world.
Instead I got to do what I came there to do,
which was sit in my little attic apartment and
work on my book.

There's not a lot of space for a writer in cul-
tures like that when you don't share the same
kind of doubt, when you like your work and
can execute it. It upsets me to think about this,
because I know other baby writers who are the
way I was, needing so many things and thinking a writing community like that might help,
but too certain for the crowd. I wasn't the kind
of writer they wanted there. I was alone and
they made sure I knew it. I remember emailing my MFA cohort to tell them about my
surgery, how major it was, how I would still
make sure I turned in my workshop notes on
time—I didn't want anyone to miss out on the
support for their work that I thought we were
there to provide for each other. I remember
how no one responded, not even a perfunctory
hope your surgery goes well. It was such an

effective way to remind me that none of them gave a fuck about me. I hadn't done anything other than face my work and try to fit in until I stopped trying, other than finish my manuscript and sign with an agent after my first year, when we were expected to do all that in our final year. Isn't it interesting, the things we can be punished for?

Anyway, that was when I hit you up to ask you if you knew anyone who could help me drive my car down to Brooklyn. We were acquaintances at best, but your network was far larger than mine and I was desperate. I hadn't expected the recovery to be so brutal, and I was alone up there, swollen and stitched up, missing an organ from my abdomen. I remember your shock at what was happening to me, the speed at which you told me you were coming to help. We didn't know each other like that, but you took a four-hour bus up from Brooklyn in the dead of winter, you made me porridge, you stayed for days, taking care of me. I couldn't even walk. I asked you why you would do all this for someone you barely knew, and you said, "We all we got."

I didn't know I could pledge loyalty to

someone that quickly and wholeheartedly, but then again, I've met very few people with a heart as kind as yours. I'm so glad you came up that week, because it reminded me that everything the cohort had done, everything the school and faculty had done to me, none of it mattered, you know? They weren't important, except as examples of where not to stay, what worlds to not bother trying to assimilate into. Ann always says, go where you are loved, and often that place has been in the dazzling warmth of your spirit. Part of bending the world we want into existence is that we get to choose who we want to be in it with, and I choose you.

You remind me, every time we talk, about the future I see for myself. I had gotten so used to pretending to be unsure because it made other people more comfortable. My first year in that MFA, the Black guy in my cohort made fun of me for videotaping my first reading. I told him that either it was going to go well and then I'd have archival footage of myself, or it would go badly and I could study it to become better. Later, he apologized. "You take yourself seriously as an artist," he said.

If there's a reputation I want to have, honestly, it's something like that. I've been to a few writer's workshops, and the thing I do of centering my work above everything else—including socializing with other writers—seems to annoy people, even when they hide it under false humor. A writer in Ghana confronts me at dinner to tell me I'm making them look bad because I wrote a few thousand words in a day. She's joking, but she's not joking. Later, she starts a nasty rumor that I was fucking one of the guys at the workshop. It's neither plausible nor interesting—it would have made way more sense to start a rumor about me and the woman writer I spent nearly all my time with at the same workshop. Neither of us drank and we both just wanted to write while we were there, instead of gossip or socialize, plus our rooms were literally next to each other's. Some people have no imagination.

I wonder how I came across in those spaces—arrogant, maybe, but unfriendly? I don't know. Spiky, perhaps, or standoffish. Armored. Set apart, certainly, because I did that myself. People can say a lot about me, but everyone knows the work is my beginning. I work

myself like it's a madness and maybe it is. It's
how I worldbend: it is my hammer, my heated
metal, my anvil, my forge, my weapon. It takes
such exertion to pretend to be unsure, and I
love how whenever I slip into it around you,
you call it out and shred it to pieces. I want to
be as brilliant as you see me. I think that is one
of the best gifts we can give each other, to hold
space for the stars that we are in each other's
eyes. When you call me from the hotel room
in Germany before your performance lecture
so I can remind you that you don't need to
prep or write things down because this work
is in your bones, you are your grandfather's
blood, all you need to do is speak from your
center and we all know there is no fear allowed
there. It stays at the periphery, where we can
ignore it, where it doesn't interfere with the
worlds we're bending into being.

Even after my MFA experience, I still tried
to find writing community. Loneliness will
drive you to that. There was a whole separate
summer workshop full of Black writers, where
I talked about how hurtful and fucked-up shit
got at the school, and the silence that followed

was especially nauseating because I thought I'd be safe among other Black writers. I didn't realize you're not supposed to talk about powerful writers like that, not publicly, as if you're not afraid of what could happen to your career.

And yet, Kathleen, I've learned so much from you about being brave. I remember when you stepped back from social media, because everyone treated you like a pit bull they could send out to attack power that they were too scared to attack themselves, hiding behind your force, instead of standing beside you in solidarity. You left them alone, and you were right to; they wanted you to be their weapon just because you don't move with fear at your center. That's the best way to worldbend, without fear. We still feel it, but we don't let it restrain us. I watched you quit your job and pack up your apartment in Bushwick, the window garden of dried flowers and fairy lights, to listen to your grandfather speaking to you from the other side, urging you to go back to Tanzania and make that work, you archivist of an artist. I can't wait to see your video installation, to hear you singing those work songs in Sukuma, to witness the world you bent by following a call.

As I get bigger and accumulate more power, I have trouble seeing myself. I still play small, out of habit and comfort. Remind me of what I am, please. I will remind you of what you are too: something magnificent, someone who makes the world bow under her hands, who pulls history out from shadows and makes people look at the hard things. And we will keep doing this for each other, world in and world out.

We all we got.

Maps | Dear Toni

This letter isn't for you.

I don't mean the public persona of you, I mean the you behind the you, the one I didn't know and never met. I've read your books, but your legacy extends far beyond anything you wrote, beyond what I can touch. I hear it when Tamara talks about you: the way you shifted realities for Black Americans, for your community. If I was inside that, perhaps I would write a different letter. Still, there's something of your spirit that touched my head, so I'm writing this letter to her—that elderspirit spun from a whisper of power.

She leapt from you as surely as if you'd pulled out a rib and molded her around it, whispering things of self and legend into her ear. I wanted so badly to meet you, just so I could look for her in you, to see if I could find her in the edge of your cheekbone, the overlap of your smiles. Maybe she'd lean into your ear and introduce us; only a spirit could, after all, us being what we are. She saw my work so clearly, and I knew you would, too. You knew about the dark folds of people, their sliding underbellies, and you spoke about looking at these things without blinking. So many people are too afraid to look. You gave me permission to lean into the terrible, of both myself and the people I wrote into existence.

Up in Syracuse, I took a seminar on your work with your friend Janis Mayes. In her classroom, I saw how agitated your work made the other students—because you wrote people who did horrific things, but you didn't tell the reader how to feel about these people. "What are we supposed to think?" one of them asked, visibly upset. "What is Morrison saying about this?"

"You figure out what you think about it," Professor Mayes said with a smile, and I was delighted. So, you could just show a terrible thing and let the showing be the strength of it? I thought it was brilliant.

The elderspirit of you leapt into my head the day Professor Mayes played a VHS tape from her archive of an interview you gave after you won the Nobel Prize. "I stood at the border, stood at the edge, and claimed it as central," you said, your voice weighted with intent. "Claimed it as central and let the rest of the world move over to where I was."

Your words reached like an arm of fire out of that television screen, and I swear they were just for me. This is the you I know. It is no small thing to give a being like me language. I had never heard or read that quote of yours before—in fact, it took me a long time to find a transcript of that interview, so that I could pull those lines out and write them down myself. For years, video of it wasn't readily available. When I used the quote, people would try to correct me. "That's from **The Paris Review,** right?" they'd say, and they'd cite a different quote. Earlier this year a clip of the video went viral and I finally found the full footage on YouTube. People all over the internet are sharing that clip now, but it cuts off before the part I think of as mine. Territorial, I know, but if you knew the kind of spirit I am, it would make sense.

See, no one makes maps for things like me. I didn't know how I was going to enter the literary world; I didn't even know if I was going to survive much more of this embodiment, to be quite honest. But then you gave me that quote, touched my head with your spirit, and I realized there didn't need to be a map, because I wasn't going anywhere. All I needed to do was stand exactly where I was, name that the center, and refuse to move.

It was one thing to do that while writing **Freshwater,** but it was a whole different beast once the book was entering the world. I remember they sent you a copy; I cannot imagine how many books you get. I wrote you a note anyway, on a card with a watercolor peach on the front. Suddenly, the career I had

dreamed of was hanging low and sweet before me. My sister and I did a photo shoot at
a bookshop for a full-page spread in **Vogue.** I
listened to Annie Leibovitz give my sister pho-
tography tips, and afterward I got her to buy
one of Helen Oyeyemi's books. It felt easy. I
knew what was going to happen with my career if I let it.

Everyone thought I was a woman. I could be
great. They thought my book was a metaphor
for mental illness. You only get one debut. **I
could be great.**

I listened to her, that elderspirit, to you.
I wrote an essay disclosing that I wasn't a
woman, that I wasn't even human, explaining
some of what an ọgbanje is. When the press
for **Freshwater** began, I made NPR acknowledge my multiplicity of self on air, made the
press use plural pronouns, centered Igbo ontology as a valid reality made unreal only by
colonialism. I repeated your words, that quote
I hunted and wrote down, in every interview
I gave. I taught it in indie bookstores, at book
festivals, in the New York Public Library and
the Schomburg. Publicly and privately, I amplified it until those lines took on a beating

heart of their own. Let the world move over, you said, and I obeyed.

The unspoken part of that is that it means I cannot move; I cannot give ground or go to them. I must hold.

It is so much harder than it sounds.

What are the costs? I wonder what you paid for that lesson. I might never know some of what has been levied against me for claiming these centers. But I believe that our centers matter, that there were people out there who needed to know that their centers mattered. People like me: embodied but not human, terrified that they're going mad, unable to talk about it, and estranged from the indigenous Black realities that might make some sense of it all. Would I have died by now if I didn't know what I was? I don't think so, but I know I would have suffered even more than I already have, and that is a terrifying thought.

You understood better than most how we're expected to move toward a certain center, to acknowledge it as the most powerful, twist our tongues toward it, hold up mirrors so it can see itself (it's narcissistic like that), scold it if we must, but center it, always center it. And if we don't, well—I don't need to tell you all this, you quite literally wrote the book. My point is, it was terrifying to hold where I was, but your voice was strong and sure.

My debut went well. The work did what it was supposed to do. I'm shedding all these faces I thought I had to wear to survive. I'm exploring the idea of deepening what I know of where I stand, where I have claimed as center.

Since I'm not moving, how can I love on where I'm standing? Who can I stand with? How do we link arms? How do we counsel each other past the fear of being deviant, since we declared these rogue centers? How do we brace against the backlash? There is so much work to be done.

But look, you gave me a spell that I am using to become free. The only map I am making is the one within myself. I am translating less and less, and my writing is better for it. I'm trying to ignore the parts that sting—the consequences of choosing a certain full brilliance. You were exemplary. I know the work I have to do. I don't know if you'd be proud of me, we never met, but it doesn't matter. You already gave me everything I needed, and I am so grateful.

This letter isn't for you. You don't need it; you're already everything. It's for all of us, those whose heads you touched. You should see my centers, Ms. Morrison. They're glorious. They pull with the force of a planet and I'm patient; it's only a matter of time.

I'm just waiting on the world.

Muse | Dear Nonso

This letter is a naming that can be spelled as a warning.

I don't think it will teach or save you from anything, but it might help you recognize something when it is happening. It is always important to see things as they are, not the masks that other people portray them to be.

I once had an affair with a married man. The married part is not important for this letter, and honestly neither is he, except as an example of the type of person I want to tell you about, so you know them when they find you, because they will find you. You are too young, too lonely, too talented. They know what we smell like, they hunt us down. He targeted me because his best friend was shielding me from him and he wanted to know who I was, why she would take international trips with me but never introduce us, why she kept me so separate. Looking back, I think she knew how hungry he was, I think she was protecting me. He finally found me at an event he knew I was attending, and it took me two years to get away from him.

Despite all the harm he carried in his hands, he also believed in me as a writer, as much as you can believe that the sun is hot, even when it doesn't know it's a sun. He paid my submission fees and set daily writing assignments for me, read everything I wrote and essentially became a mentor to me—that is, the sort of mentor who was also fucking me and cheating on his wife. Their baby was a few months old. "All you have to do is master your craft," he would tell me, "and then no one can touch you. That's how talented you are." He was controlling and abusive and he saw my power years before I saw it myself. His ex-girlfriend was an incredibly famous artist whose studio he took me to. "She can buy your whole village," he told me, "but never doubt that you are her peer." It sounded preposterous then. I see what he meant now.

I want to warn you about people like him, men like him. They want you to become powerful, yes, but the secret is that you were **already** powerful. They know entities like us are afraid of our own strength, afraid of unfolding into a world like this. They know how lonely we are, how starved we are, and they swoop down on us. He was sixteen years older than I was, he called himself my senior brother, and he raped me in my shower. He wanted me to stay a child forever, young and wide-eyed, scared but excited, sharing the world with him as I saw it for the first time with my new soft eyes. These men are always like that. They want you to desire their approval, their validation, to feed them a bright stream of love and support and the sheer drug that is belief, the engine that is belief, the catalyst that is belief. You're not supposed to grow up or outgrow them, to reach a place where they have more to learn from you than to teach you. You're supposed to be sticky with amber, gazing at them as it sets, settling you into a brilliant stillness. They deeply value your mind, but as a resource, as a glittering mine.

You're not supposed to know how brilliant you are. You are absolutely not supposed to know how much they are in awe of you, because if you saw yourself as the large and beastly thing you are, you would see them too. And they cannot bear to be seen, Nonso— not because you'd think any less of them, but perhaps precisely because you wouldn't. Oh, there is a trap of hierarchies somewhere in this, but you are most likely a greater thinker and artist than they are. More talented, more thoughtful, more skilled. It matters and it doesn't, but it matters to them. Most things are about power. If a beast like you gazes up at them in adoration, then what a beast **they** must be, just from the strength of your eyes. You still hold the power, but you're not supposed to know that. A god with a collar around their throat, adoring a human; a god who doesn't know they're a god, or who knows and puts it aside just for this human. Is a muse a servant?

They need you to think they are more powerful than you, because that is literally the only thing **making** them more powerful than you. You dispense the anointing oil, you are the power. What you say, goes. If you say they are your superior, then it becomes real only because you said it. If you say you are bigger than they are, then that is also real, and they know this.

So you see, it is important that you say the right thing. It is important to them because you make them, and you can just as easily unmake them.

I have unmade a few people in my time. There was another man, this one twenty-seven years older than me, respected and popular in certain Black art circles. He spent months trying to hook me in and I sidestepped his approaches, disappearing into Trinidad, rejecting his offers. I think he was so used to being revered by young Black artists, he didn't expect my indifference. He was, as they always are, so hungry. I think they are lonely, too, you know? It's a shame they decide to be violent with it. He finally brought an offering I accepted and we met in person, working on a brief shoot together. He offered to make a thirty-second book trailer for **Freshwater,** but then he read it and went ablaze with ideas, expanding the project into a fifteen-minute piece. He recorded me speaking about the work for four hours straight, he flew me to LA often and paid for everything. He took me to galas and retreats, and I thought we were friends because this is precisely what I'd do for my friends— spoil them rotten, fly them places to be with me. By this time the magician and I were already lovers, and I had no interest in hooking up with this man. When I pointed out to him that all the other artists assumed we were fucking, he said it was unnecessary to correct them. When he eventually professed his feelings for me, they were ravenous. I was an engine for his mind, a world he could not access on his own, a thing he had never seen before. I, meanwhile, was fascinated by his fascination with me. He spent days investigating my work, my mind, my practice. Over time, however, his facade started fraying. I would see his irritation when I disagreed with him, when I pushed back, when I didn't play the role I was supposed to.

Freshwater was about to come out and we were meant to shoot the video piece together, then debut it online as part of the book launch. On my last trip to LA with him, he showed me another project he was working on for a friend and flippantly mentioned that it didn't matter what the friend did, because he (this man) was going to sell it through his gallery for hundreds of thousands of dollars. It wasn't until I'd flown back to New York, and was on the phone with Chinelo, that it hit me that he saw our project the same way: he was only collaborating with me so he could sell the final piece as his work and his work alone. I feel sick even typing this out, remembering how calculating he was, for months and months. The flattery, the gifts, stripping down at his stylist friend's house, the shopping: Rick Owens. Margiela. Ann Demeulemeester. It was all a fucking trap.

I called my agent immediately. She reassured me that, in order for him to sell any video work based on **Freshwater,** he would have to acquire the option for the book. Armed with this information, I called and kept my voice sweet and innocent, playing the naive artist with overprotective reps, shifting power so he wouldn't be able to tell that I could see what he was. "My agents just want to confirm that we're not making this piece for profit," I said. "We're just releasing it online like we said, right?"

He paused. He was on his way to the gym. When his voice came through the phone again, he was telling me how he needed to sell it in order to make back the money he was investing into the piece. "I'm spending twenty thousand dollars," he said, his voice swelling with manufactured indignation. "If your agents want money back from this, then they should invest in it as well."

This was just days before I was meant to fly back to LA for the two-day shoot. We talked for a few more minutes and I pointed out that the entire piece was based on me and my book.

It was my intellectual work, my voice, my flesh on camera. That has worth, I reminded him gently.

"You're right," he said. "Let me think about it."

"Sure," I replied, charm a liar in my cheek. "Call me later."

As soon as he got off the phone, I blocked him on every single mode of communication. I called my agents back and formally burned my relationship with him down to the ground. I removed him from my book launch schedule, pulling him from an event, and severed every agreement, every tie, everything. This forced him to go through my agents; he was never able to contact me directly after that. I saw a glimpse of an email he sent them, alleging that I was "mistaken" about his intention to sell the work. I told them it was unnecessary to copy me on any emails about him. I vanished back into myself. Weeks later, Ann retrieved my suitcase from his house in LA. He'd left the Rick Owens coat and the Demeulemeester boots folded neatly inside.

Nonso, this man was so bold—he was going to steal my work, sell it for six figures, and cut me out of the process entirely. Can you imagine? I don't even blame him for wanting to be in a relationship with me; where better to keep your muse than close to you, blind to you, so you can extract endlessly from them? I was still so scared, back then. You have to remember that **Freshwater** was just about to come out, so I was already wrecked with anxiety over that, decimated by stress and fear, my entire future hinging on the success of this work, and I had just destroyed what so many other artists would have considered a hugely beneficial relationship. The minute I removed this man from my book event, the moderator pulled out as well—they'd agreed to do the event for free to support Black art, but his clout was the actual currency, I suppose. I was terrified that he would find a way to come at me for cutting off his access so brutally, but I couldn't have done anything other than what I did. My fear doesn't matter in the face of protecting the work. What was the alternative, to gaslight myself into thinking I was mistaken, to let him continue with his plan, to pretend he wasn't trying to exploit my work for his own career? It was my first book, no one knew me yet.

The rules are clear, no matter the stakes: when anyone fucks with the work, **burn them to the ground.**

You know, he used to tell me he was used to being the weirdest person in the room, and I was confused, because he was so terribly ordinary. I wonder how many more of them are out there, boring people who can only summon up a glamour around themselves if they siphon it from someone else. What I'm trying to say is, be careful of these hungry ones, Nonso, but also, don't worry. You will always be more powerful than they are, even if it takes you a while to remember it, to unfold into your full self. No human can anoint you or take your anointing away. They will try everything to make you believe that the power lies with them, that you have to remain in their favor, that they are strong enough to shift your destiny, but that's impossible. If you say yes with enough force, your chi will say yes, too. It will clear the road for you like the hand of God. You are always who you are, you see. No one else can make you. And when the hungry ones come, don't worry even if you fall into the trap, we are lonely and we have our own appetites.

Nothing can hold you for long. Just remember that you are the one who makes worlds, and you are the one who can burn them down.

Gore | Dear Senthuran

The first time I met you, we sat in the café on Malcolm X that doesn't exist anymore and talked about eating people, carving them up in tender moments, swallowing their meat and gristle. You were writing your second book, **Rot (Hunger),** and it sounded wonderful, a thing rooted in cannibalism. I remember that you wore a black turtleneck and smelled of cigarette smoke, the way my ex-husband used to. I told you it was a writer stereotype, your look, your smoking. You assured me that, true to form, you'd been drinking whiskey the night before, and we laughed. I started the idea of this book when we exchanged emails, simply because I like the way your name sounds. It fits after a **dear,** it sounds like it wants letters written to it. After that café, I also liked the way your mind works. I was glad you were the one translating **Freshwater** into German. Someone who understands—or at the very least, is interested in—this kind of consumption is a good fit.

The magician joined us halfway at the café, in the pastel booth. The year before, he'd walked me through Central Park with my eyes closed. I get overwhelmed in the city sometimes; there are too many people, too many humans pushing through the air. With his hand in mine all I had was sound, sifting its way through dappled darkness. I was a little scared as I walked, and his touch was the only thread pulling me through the world. Eventually the sounds of people faded, and when he asked me to open my eyes the first time, we were standing under trees, a woodland around us. All the people had evaporated, lost to clouds, and the only sound was that of the birds. I didn't know you could be this alone in Central Park. The magician made birdsong with his mouth and the birds mimicked him and I watched, as delighted as a child.

He asked me to close my eyes again and we walked some more. After some minutes, he stopped me and turned me around, then helped me to the ground. I could feel grass under my palms, brushing the back of my neck. I had just turned thirty. When I opened my eyes, the sky was an unreasonable amount of blue above me, streaked with white clouds. We were in an empty meadow. I think that afternoon was when I started to fall in love with him.

I'd brought leftover birthday cake—he'd been at my birthday party on Christine's Bed-Stuy rooftop, but he'd had to leave before we cut the cake I named Victory. It took me two days to make—Victory was a five-layer lemon olive oil cake soaked in rosemary syrup, filled with alternating layers of blackberry curd and a strawberry basil filling. It had dollops of vegan lemon buttercream between each layer, drips of strawberry royal icing, and I'd painted it with gold shimmer, put pink sugar pearls and candied rosemary and thirty gold candles on it. Half the ingredients I bought at the Woolies in Jozi when I was there with Eloghosa. Victory tells you a lot about who I am as a god, things about decadence, making something beautiful just so it can be consumed and destroyed. The magician ate it from aluminum foil and looked at me like I had put a world on his tongue.

We sat in the meadow for a long time, and he laid his head on my thighs while I stroked his shaved head. His eyes were closed, and the sun broke against his face. I wondered what it would be like to make an incision at the top of his forehead, a neat and curved line hooking behind his ears, the exhale of blood that would bead up then rivulet past his eyebrows, into the hollows of his eye sockets, pooling until it submerged his lashes. I'd peel his scalp back and the blood would coat my thighs before being swallowed by the grass. It would be wet and red under his skin, maybe with glimpses of bone, the mad pulsing of an exposed vein. I wondered if he would know how sweetly I meant it, how tender the skinning would be, how close it would make us, having the flap of his skin in my hand. It took me weeks before

I told him about this fantasy—I wasn't sure what he was at first, how he'd respond, if he would understand. He did.

He'd offer me his arm. A hand. The hollow of his rib cage if I wanted to break open his sternum and curl up against his flailing lungs. Sharp teeth breaking my skin. Flayings. Corpses. When he was in college, he used to do brandings. I've been branded once, by a man in Massachusetts at a tattoo parlor. It's a perfect circle on my right shoulder, darker in the middle, a hypertrophic scar right above the one from my polio vaccination. The metal rod that made it was oh so slender, heated so hot. When it was pressed into my skin, I smelled flesh roasting, cooked meat. Then the nerves burned off and I felt nothing. I would let the magician carve spells into me. I've carved spells into myself. We described falling in love as if we both reached into each other's chest, up to the elbow, an intrusive intimacy we couldn't twist away from, pinned to each other like insects. As with impalements, if you ripped our arms out of each other, would we bleed to death?

The point was that it hurt, that our fingers

were lost in a forest of sluicing flesh, nerves raked under the fingernails, a heart pounding against a palm, desperate ventricles, you know? It's only a small step from impaling someone to devouring them, you're already in there.

At the café, we talked about Sada Abe and the Rotenburg Cannibal. I didn't ask if you'd ever wanted someone enough to cut them, to eat them. We didn't know each other like that; we still don't. But I wonder how personal those interests are for you—if it's a love language in your mouth, too, this terribly Catholic thing of eating the flesh and drinking the blood. Isn't that such ritualistic dedication? Every week, to line up, to swallow a wound in the side, a flood from the wrists, the top of the foot, flavored with the wood of the cross, thousands of years in vintage. I wonder what other parts of the Christ we'd be eating. The soft of his lower lip. A strip of his bellyskin. A thin slice from his inner thigh. His body, dividing endlessly like bread, like fish. Where was the blood drained from? Was it rich in oxygen, a bright bubbling red? Was it dark, deep, gasping?

Don't even get me started on vampires.

When I mentioned Sada Abe to Tiona, she

talked about **Beloved,** Sethe wanting to eat someone's cheek—which is some Hannibal Lecter shit, but then again, imagine the kind of intimacy with Lecter! There's a sensuality there, that he would kill you, prepare and then consume you, and isn't that also sexy? There's something deliberate there, something patient and thought out, unhurried. Don't we deserve someone who puts us in their mouth slowly?

As for Sada Abe—look, I get her wanting to kill her lover, strangling him to death like she did, that makes sense. But the organ she picked? It's just not what I would've chosen. There's nothing interesting about a penis once you separate it from the body—it's just a tube of tissue, really. There are so many organs you could pick with far more appeal—like do you know how wet lungs are? Or how slippery the liver is, just lobes and lobes of it sliding between your fingers. I like the lungs, though, because they hang. And when you run your fingers over the ridges of the trachea and the bronchi, you can feel how essential they are, both rigid and soft. I think I was eighteen when they let me cut into a cadaver in undergrad, and it was just wonderful, taking him apart. And then in vet school, when they let me cut into dead animals—you know, part of why I quit was because I had no interest in keeping the thing I was dissecting alive. It didn't really matter, that wasn't the point. You had to learn so much to keep them alive, how tedious. What was important was the cutting, the opening, the peeling. My roommate Emily, a petite white girl who used to be a dancer, told me that it scared her to watch me cut. "You're so fixated on it," she said. "I feel like I'm going to wake up one night and find you cutting me."

I wouldn't have cut her. She wasn't my type. And if I was to cut someone, or cut something off someone, I'd rather cut something out of someone. The penis just hangs on the outside, you don't even get to dig for it! You don't get to search for it, you don't get to dive or probe or reach for it, where is the effort, where is the dedication, where's the fun? There's just so much more potential in other places. I'm partial to chest cavities over abdominal ones. Everything's all smushed together in the abdomen, I feel. You've just got meters and meters of gut—for what? But in the chest, it's so neat, it's structured and caged and you can break things apart and you can follow the flow. There's a way to dissect a heart where it just blossoms like a peony in your hands and you can see everything inside. You can close it and open it and that, I think, is a gift.

The other night, I asked the magician, "Have you ever thought of skinning me?"

"Of course," he said. "Skinning you and wearing you."

"I wouldn't fit," I pointed out. There's not enough of my skin to make a shirt for him. We'd shared pictures and stories of books bound in human hide earlier that week.

"I don't need all of you to fit," he replied. "I'd make a cockring out of your skin, so you would always be close to me."

That, I think, is intimacy, a gentle and maddened kind of love. I figured you might understand.

Money | Dear Nonso

This letter is a record; I want to be transparent about as much of this industry as I can. Publishing can be so opaque, so human, full of invisible rules. I hope this record is helpful to writers coming after me. I would not have the space to be safe, to focus on unfolding as a self, if not for the money.

It's that simple and ugly: the secret is usually money. Time, as well, but you can buy that.

I was able to be so prolific from the start because I was fully funded for the first two years of my career. In the fall of 2014, I entered an

MFA program that paid me a stipend for my first year. I wrote **Freshwater** during those two semesters, in a small attic apartment with my mattress on the floor. There was so much time. All we did was read stories and talk and write. I dropped out after my third semester, but in my first summer there I signed with the Wylie Agency.

Afterward, one of the faculty members walked me through the publication process, hypothesizing that my debut novel might sell for ninety thousand dollars, which blew my mind. Here was a rich, successful writer, suggesting that I would make more money than I'd ever had in my life, **for a single book.** Surely he knew enough about the industry, surely his estimate was realistic. Looking back, he was probably assuming that I would stay and graduate from the program; or maybe his estimate was for people who looked like him, maybe it would only apply if I was a white male writer with an MFA. I was assumed to be a woman, a Black one, an African. I don't think many of the people at that institution thought I'd get to where I am now, especially not after I walked out, but I couldn't have stayed. There's no separation between my professional life and my spirit life, they are the same thing. Nothing was allowed to come before the work—not power, not money, not institutional politics. All that mattered was that I took care of the book, that I became a stronger writer so I could keep telling these stories. Anything that got in the way of that had to be burned down, so I burned it down.

While I was still in the program, the faculty discouraged me from applying to other opportunities, hinting that my MFA funding could be pulled. I just smiled and nodded, then continued with my applications. I had no intention of being trapped there, of having their funding used as a choke collar to keep me compliant. In my second year I was expected to serve as a teaching assistant, but the job gave me panic attacks, so I had to stop. At first they reassured me that they'd just find another position for me, this happened often, it was no problem, but then they couldn't find one, so they started to pressure me to drop out or take a medical leave. My major depression was already registered with the school as a psychological disability, so they couldn't fire me;

the only way they could stop paying me was if I left voluntarily. It always goes back to the money. I refused to leave. It wasn't time yet.

The one Black faculty member took me out to lunch. "If you can't handle this program, you should drop out," he told me. I refused. They were supposed to find me a job I could do without jeopardizing my health, I told him. I was fine. I just couldn't teach. He became agitated, raising his voice, leaning across the table to yell at me. "So you're not fragile? You're not actually fragile?!" The year before, he'd taught me that my future archive existed in the work I was doing now. "Save everything," he'd said. "Let the grad students sort it out later."

I stayed, stubborn in my brutal fragility. I collected my checks. The other students avoided me, and I stayed, waiting for the right time to leave. All my relationships with faculty had soured. I was working as a personal assistant to another famous writer in the program; she'd been so proud when I signed to Wylie, but when I tried telling her about the isolation, her tone changed. "It's probably just in your head," she said. "You know you have depression." Shortly after, she let me go from

the position. I'd been trying to figure out how
to quit, so I didn't mind. I was just glad I got
to keep the iPad she'd bought me because I
couldn't afford to replace it. I'm telling you all
this, Nonso, because it connects back to the
money, to the choices I've had to make in this
industry that followed spirit and not human
sense. I'm fine now, but it was ugly then. I was
walking away from a fully funded spot at an
MFA program with prestigious faculty. None
of them would ever write me a recommenda-
tion letter. I didn't know how the industry
worked, so I was constantly terrified that they
would blackball me, that my career would die
because I'd refused to fall in line and I'd never
make any money as a writer. **Freshwater** was
out on submission and every editor was passing on it. I was so fucking scared, but like I've
said before, this whole thing is between me
and God, not between me and humans. It felt
like a road leading to a future I couldn't see
yet, but I could feel God telling me that all I
had to do was stay on the road, stay obedient,
no matter the costs.

During that last semester, I made the short-
list for the Miles Morland Scholarship, and

they sent me a list of interview questions for their next round of decisions. I told them how I was leaving my MFA program with no plan. I had no money, I would lose my apartment, and all I wanted was to focus on my work. I didn't know what else to say other than the truth. When I got the news that they were awarding me a scholarship, I cried and cried. It was a week after my hysterectomy and I could barely walk, but I'd stepped out into nothingness only to be caught by the grace of God. For the whole of 2016, the foundation would pay me £18,000 in monthly disbursements to write **The Death of Vivek Oji.** I could live anywhere I wanted, do anything I wanted; all they required was that I turn in ten thousand words each month. In this world, money buys both time and freedom. I'm sure you know that already.

I waited until I collected my January check from the MFA program, then told them I was dropping out. After packing up my attic apartment, I crashed with a Nigerian friend in Brooklyn who refused to let me pay him rent. "Save your money," he said, and he moved his office out into his dining room so I could use the spare bedroom. I slept and wrote in that room for five months. When May came, I flew to Vietnam with a complete manuscript, sending it out in ten-thousand-word chunks for the rest of the year. I was at my grandmother's house in Malaysia when we finally got an offer from a publisher for **Freshwater,** six months after we'd sent it out. It was for ten thousand dollars.

I was devastated.

Don't get me wrong, I hadn't been expecting much, certainly not the ninety thousand dollars I'd heard back in the MFA program. This is America, after all, and **Freshwater** was drenched in obscure Igbo ontology. The closest novel you could compare it to was maybe Ben Okri's **The Famished Road,** and even then you'd still be miles away. I thought I was okay with being unseen. There was a private dinner once at the school, with three famous white writers, and I remember sitting there listening to their lives and stories. At some point I thought, if this is what people want to read, there's a strong chance that my work will never find a home in this country. My worlds were so far away from that dinner table. I wanted to be back at my apartment, working, instead of sitting there listening to a foreign kind of glory.

So I had tempered my hopes to a level I thought was more reasonable for an unknown African writer who hadn't managed to get published in any literary journals or U.S. publications. Maybe thirty thousand dollars? Forty thousand if I was lucky? Even after the ten-thousand-dollar offer came in, I thought we could try to get it bumped up. A twenty-thousand-dollar advance wouldn't be bad; I could make it stretch. When Jackie made a counteroffer, though, it was rejected. This was as high as they were willing to go. I didn't feel like I had a choice. It was either take this offer and publish the book, or hold off—and then what? Try again later? There was no later, there was only now.

It was already terrifyingly obvious that editors didn't know what to do with this book, that they liked the writing but didn't know how to market it. Maybe I was too unknown for work this risky, where no one knew how it would sell because there wasn't really precedent for it in the market. Maybe if I'd written something easier, something safer. Maybe if I didn't insist on walking everywhere aflame. Years before, Enuma told me to go with the story that scared me, and I still do that, I still run toward the fear.

Jackie and I accepted the offer. I didn't know what to do with my feelings. I was glad that the book was being published, of course, and by an editor willing to take a chance on it, but I was so fucking sad about the advance. It felt like all my fears about publishing as an African writer in the U.S., as a Black writer talking about metaphysical shit, about how much I'd be undervalued—they had all come true. I felt like I wasn't worth shit. Like my work wasn't worth shit. I didn't even know how I was going to pay my rent or survive for the next year or two. I had funding through December, but I didn't know what I'd do after that. I moved to Trinidad that fall, budgeting to stay there for a year, but after my roommate nearly got us evicted, I found myself paying for a two-bedroom apartment alone and my savings vanished.

I left after only six months and lived out of my suitcases for most of 2017, staying with friends, traveling because it was cheaper than paying rent, unable to afford a lease. A residency in Bulgaria. Commonwealth Writers in Singapore. Six weeks with Kathleen in Dar es Salaam. It looked marvelous on Instagram, and it was hellish offline. In August I finally made it back to Brooklyn, crashed on a friend's couch for a few weeks, then started dragging my suitcases from sublet to sublet, watching as I ran out of money. Earlier that year I'd received a $5,000 grant from the Astraea Foundation for my video work, and that—along with the sectioned payments of my advance, and some money from translation deals for **Freshwater**—kept my head afloat.

By October, though, I was distraught. I had no money and no place to live once my sublet expired. I refused to get a job. There was just no fucking way I was waiting tables again or writing cover letters. I had promised myself that back in 2014, when I left my nonprofit job for the MFA and started writing full time. I had even tattooed my knuckles to make myself unemployable, to remind myself that I was a spirit and none of this shit applied to me. I wrote books. That was my work, and either that paid me or—there wasn't actually anything after that. It had to pay me. I would bend the world if I had to, but it had to pay me.

Back in 2016, Chris Myers had asked me to write a YA novel for his new imprint at Random House. I'd refused because I had a list of books I already wanted to write and a YA novel wasn't on the list. He'd told me that all I needed to make a YA sale to him was the first thirty pages and a one-page proposal for the rest of the book. In the terrible fall of 2017, I'd been telling him about all the trouble I was having, and he suggested we have lunch to talk it out more. I figured he would bring up the YA novel again, and this time, it looked like a lifeline. I sat down and wrote the first two chapters of **Pet** in a day, printed them out, and took them to the restaurant, giving them to him to read. He loved the book and I sold it to Make Me a World, his imprint, for forty thousand dollars. I was starting to realize how straightforward this industry could be—if all I had to do was write books, then sell them.

I finished **Pet** in two months, turning it in that December, still waiting anxiously for the contract to be signed, then for the first part of my advance to be processed. **Freshwater** was slated to publish in February 2018, but as of that January, I didn't even have money to pay my rent. That was when I decided: I would never do the edits before receiving the check. It wasn't worth it.

That's also when my human mother was upset because I wasn't "excited" enough about my book launch, wasn't "sharing this moment with my family," but the truth is that I was horribly depressed and stressed out—something very few people could see, because all they saw was my dream coming true. It took six months for me to get editorial notes from the publisher, much longer than I'd anticipated or budgeted for; I'd been counting on the second part of the advance, which was due on acceptance of my revised manuscript, but I couldn't deliver it without getting the edits. Learning the timing of this industry is a brutal lesson: we're really still just freelancers waiting for salaried people to pay us what we're owed. Jackie got Random House to release enough of my advance so I could pay my rent, and that spring we started planning the sale of my next adult novel, **The Death of Vivek Oji.**

This time, I wanted to crack six figures. I

didn't know or care if this was a reasonable goal, but I wanted it. **Freshwater** had broken through; we'd gone into a third printing before publication and a fourth the month after, and it was racking up strong reviews. I told myself that if I'd been a white girl photographed by Annie Leibovitz for **Vogue** before her debut novel was even published, this wouldn't be a question. Then again, I couldn't tell if all of this was really groundbreaking or not, or if any of it would matter in selling the next book. The truth is, there's no formula for determining advances. You can set an arbitrary number; maybe someone will pay it to you, or maybe they won't.

Because my publishers were independent, I decided in advance that I would stay with them if they offered $75,000—just because it was them, just so I could keep working with my editor. I'd seen older writers talk about having the same editor for years, book after book, and there's something valuable about working with someone over an extended time, who knows your work so intimately. When we entered negotiations, though, they couldn't reach the figure I wanted. **Freshwater** hadn't hit any bestseller lists or won any awards. (The award season hadn't really even started yet, but we'd started our negotiations a few months into publication, working with what we had.)

This moment was pivotal. If we took the book out to other publishers and no one else wanted it, we'd have to come crawling back to a lower offer. In many ways, it would have been safer to stay instead of taking a gamble, but after my experience at the MFA program, I was learning to bet on myself. I also never wanted to worry about rent again, so all my sentimentality about staying with the same editor evaporated. Pay attention. Loyalty is irrelevant if you can't pay your bills. Someone who is on your side will never expect you to put aside your well-being for their sake; they will understand if you can't stay because you need to take care of yourself. My allegiance was always to my work, not to companies or institutions. This whole thing is a business, and I needed six figures.

Who was I going to believe if I didn't believe myself? I'd started to think of what I wanted my future to look like. I took a walk with the magician through Ditmas Park to look at houses, calculating how much money I'd need to be able to afford one. In five books, we thought, perhaps I could hit $250,000 for an advance, and that would give me a down payment. I met Tamara in a terrible little restaurant on Stuyvesant and showed her house listings in New Orleans, where they had smaller, more affordable versions of the Ditmas houses—and no winter. If I sold **Vivek** the way I wanted, I might be able to afford one. I could afford more later. All I had to do was write.

So I turned down my publisher's offer and Jackie sent the book out on submission. We got interest from other houses and met with five or six of them. I wore my PR mask till it stuck to my skin, stretching the corners of my mouth into a charismatic smile. I evaluated them, listening to which parts of the book made them flinch, which parts they loved, what suggestions they had around form, how big they thought I could get. I made power maps and gauged their aptitude with social media from their Instagram pages. Jackie explained that no one was allowed to make an offer until we had finished all our meetings. Remember that the money is arbitrary; it will drive you mad to try to anticipate it. You find out the range once the offers start coming in, and when Jackie sent me the first one, I sat down and stared at the email in shock.

One hundred thousand dollars.

We were **starting** at one hundred thousand dollars.

I could have cried; I was filled with a grim satisfaction. The validation was immense, an expanding cloud inside me. I had bet on myself. I had bet on **myself** and I had won. No matter what happened after this first offer, I was going to be able to buy a house. Even with no bestseller lists, no awards, no TV appearances, an amputated tour, a writer living on multiple margins in a country that is not home, writing metaphysics and queer sex, a dead thing walking, an opaque illegible entity, and **I had won.** I knew what I was doing. I had listened to myself, to the quiet godvoice inside me, instead of the stories other people had—that I needed to finish the MFA before I let my agent submit my work, that leaving the program meant losing something, that I wouldn't get anywhere without the support of that institution, that I needed that degree, that prestige, their friendship and favor, their anointing—or they would shut me out, they would slice me behind the knees, and I would fade away, unknown and too stubborn to assimilate when all I wanted was my work, the freedom and health to make it, the platforms to share it.

The next offer was for $200,000. For a single book. For Vivek and Osita and love in a dark room. I hopped on and off the phone with Jackie as the auction (a whole auction!) progressed. Another publisher matched the offer. It was happening so fast, in minutes. We were waiting to hear back from another. Would anyone go up to $250,000? Then, in what I still think of as a bit of a power move, as if to kill the back and forth, Riverhead Books made a two-book offer for $500,000. Half a million fucking dollars. I had been there, ready to sell my work for $75,000, and now someone was offering me half a million. Nonso, I swear, this world is truly a mad place.

At first, I didn't even take it. I wondered if I should just sell one book and try to get a bit more for that one, but then Jackie pointed out that it might be difficult to get $250,000 for the second book if we waited to do them separately. Besides, I figured, I already had the next one written. We accepted the offer. Two months later, I got a check for $130,000.

It was the most money I'd ever had in my life.

I paid off my credit cards, gave away thousands, spent thousands on myself. When the first royalties for **Freshwater** came in, I called my agents to make sure the amount was right. My percentage of what the book had made was $40,000, and after the advance was subtracted from that, I walked away with $30,000. Money was pouring in from foreign sales of my work, fragments of advances due on signing: £20,000 for the UK sale of **Vivek.** Ten thousand euros for the Italian sale of **Freshwater.** Ten thousand euros for the French sale. In a note on my phone, I mapped out when the rest of the advances were due, spread out over the next few years: €12,000, £10,000, $50,000, $62,500.

In the fall of 2019, I sublet a house in New Orleans from a woman who kept horses in her backyard, and then I bought a secondhand SUV for seven thousand dollars in cash. A few months later I bought a brand-new house, named it Shiny, then spent a truly ridiculous amount of money furnishing and decorating it in an unnecessarily short amount of time. I wasn't used to having money like this, and it took me a long time to learn how to manage it. My credit limits skyrocketed, and I kept putting shit on my cards because I could, because I told myself safety was never having to worry about money again. But we forget, safety is the familiar, and I was putting myself back into what I knew best, what I could commiserate with my friends about instead of leaving them behind—debt. Bassey called it a form of self-sabotage, and she was right. I've always been terrified of success. I didn't want to go back to having to budget, to having to **think** about money. It felt like freedom to be able to afford almost anything I wanted.

Maybe I needed those months to get the fear out of my system, to understand that safety didn't look like running away from restraint. Sometimes I think about how half a million isn't even that much money if you shift your eye well, but I also think that God gave me the amount of money I could handle. And of all the things to splurge on, a home in a country where I've never had a home wasn't a bad investment. It is the place I will write the rest of my books, make the rest of my money, and find a quieter type of freedom. If there's any advice I could give about all this, I'd say to bet on yourself—and, for the love of everything holy, put aside 30 percent of all your income for taxes, because that shit will fuck you over so fast. I still haven't caught up, but I'm learning to slow down.

Jackie's negotiating another book deal as I type this, for the sequels to **Pet.** We haven't settled on an amount yet, but we're already at six figures for each book. **Freshwater** is in development at FX, and if it goes to pilot, the book rights will sell for $125,000. If it goes to series, I'll make a few more hundred thousand. It's not even enough. I have $250,000 of student loans to pay off and a $300,000 mortgage. I've adjusted to thinking in six figures. I want to get to seven. I want to wipe out every penny of debt and see what it feels like to breathe then, how to start redistributing resources once I'm in the black, the thick glorious black. I know these are big numbers, but at last, they're just numbers, you know? It's just money. Besides, I'm a god.

I know this was a long letter, but it's been a long fucking road. I wanted to make a record of it, even the tedious parts, because in each step is a choice, a decision that led me here. I hope you find it useful.

Shiny | Dear Marguerite

I've been dreaming about the house I grew up in.

It's not an easy house to write about. I haven't lived there in fifteen years, and for most of them, I chose to remember the better parts. Eating suya sandwiches with my sister late at night after our father got home from the club, roasted meat and red onions between soft white bread. Every single mango season. The generations of skinny cats running through the rooms, the dogs one after another. Heidi, Rambo, then Rex. The long afternoons playing with Barbies on the rug, making an upside-down umbrella their ship. Magic, stories, and so many books. It could be such a pretty picture. If it was, maybe I wouldn't mind seeing it again when I dream.

I hate that house. It's the house where bad things first happened, the house our mother left us in, the house of our father's temper and our brother's cruelty, with the torn lino-leum and the ugly walls and the lace curtains gone brown with dust. That house made me terrified of cockroaches—they flew in my face at night, crawled on my walls and once, while I slept, up my legs. They laid eggs in the fridge and hid in the corners. I have panic attacks when I see roaches now; it's gotten bet-ter than when I used to just scream and scream, but I still spin out and cry, shaking and bab-bling to myself. I hate that house. I hate how dirty it is, the layers and layers of filth every-where. My father doesn't clean. He waits for a woman or child to do it. I still have actual nightmares about our toilet. We never had enough water. Once, my mother's best friend took us aside to ask us why there was so much shit floating in the toilet. We were conserving

water, waiting until it was absolutely necessary
to flush by pouring a bucket of dirty laundry water down the bowl. I learned shame in
that moment and I learned other things in that
house: how to be cruel, how to hurt my sister
when I was angry, how well she could learn,
too. I learned I was fat and loud and that my
anger could make me such a monster that even
my own mother was too scared to punish me.
I still dream about the open wounds on our
dog's ears, red and swollen, thick with black
flies. We couldn't heal them; we couldn't stop
the constant pain. In the dreams, the dog waits
for me at the back door with trusting eyes.

Writing this is hard because I feel guilty
about how much I hate that house when I'm
not sure if my sister feels the same way. We
used to tell stories as if our childhood memories were fused, and now this feels like it could
be another way we've split apart. Like how she
still loves our father.

I don't feel ashamed about how we grew up.
It was fine, and we didn't know anything else.
I used to say it was a wonderful childhood, and
sometimes it was. Other times, it was fucking terrible. Both can sit next to each other.

What I feel ashamed about is how viscerally I never want to go back. Not to the house, not to that past, that life, those memories. I hate that I keep dreaming about the house. The other night, I dreamed about needing to wash my hair and looking through the wardrobe I shared with my sister for the right shampoo. There were the same buckets of water in the bathroom next to the plastic storage drum and my sister was telling me to hurry up so she could take her turn. Sometimes the dream is set in our parlor, or our kitchen, or the corridor where we once played with mercury and, separately, accidentally set fire to the floor.

I want the dreams to stop. I tell myself that I'm grown up now. I don't have to ever go back there if I don't want to. I can let the house die in the past, entomb everything that's in it.

This is not a letter about my father.

MY MOTHER'S HOUSE is in Albuquerque. She's been there for more than a decade. Her little yard involves garden gnomes. She is a superhost on Airbnb. It is **her** house. We're welcome to come whenever we want and stay as long as we need, but I've never thought of it as my home. My sister lived there; she went to high school and college in Albuquerque. She's the only child who's ever lived alone with our parents—first our father, then our mother. I think it complicates her relationships with them in a way my brother and I will never quite understand. I do notice that she is kinder to them. My mother keeps a fastidiously clean house. She is tidy and very, very particular; she likes everything in her house to be a certain way and gets stressed out when it deviates too much. It's one of the things we have in common.

My mother has the same name as your mother. Katherine wondered if that was weird for you, and I suppose I do, too. You haven't talked about your mother since the summer, and I try not to ask, even though I know she died in those hot months. Katherine told me. I wonder what the house you grew up in was like.

My house in New Orleans is called Shiny the Godhouse. It's a bungalow with a large yard, which I'm cultivating into a garden. I bought it in March 2019, four months after I quietly started living between New Orleans and Brooklyn. I thought I was going to end up buying a different house, a duplex that I'd have to gut and remodel. I fixated on interior design, watching home renovations shows, spending hours and hours on the internet, sketching out rooms, ordering tile samples. Kathleen came down for Christmas and we compared tile combinations: emerald-green zellige tiles for the kitchen walls, terra-cotta hex tile for the floor, mother-of-pearl in the bathroom. I couldn't actually buy a house until my taxes were done, because my income wasn't real until then, no matter how much money sat in my bank accounts. I had to wait, and after all that waiting, I didn't end up with the duplex. It would've cost too much to renovate it, to convert it into the five-bedroom house I was dreaming about.

Instead, my real estate agent started showing me other houses, trying to figure out what I wanted. The finishes were a big deal for me; I wanted beautiful tile and real hardwood floors, a house where I wouldn't have to rip out the backsplash and change the countertops. We came close a few times, but there was always something wrong, something I would've had to compromise on. The ceilings were too low. The floor was too dark. The bathroom tile was ugly. The stove was electric, not gas. I didn't want to settle.

We were looking over listings one evening when he spotted a house. "This one," he said. "We have to go look at it right now." It was already dark outside, but he called the selling agent and we drove over to the house, letting ourselves in with the key in the lockbox.

As soon as I stepped inside, I knew.

The house had enormous windows and high ceilings, a gorgeous hardwood floor, and a kitchen island that I hugged immediately. It had three bedrooms and all of them had walk-in closets. It had an office, a laundry room, and floor-to-ceiling marble in both the bathrooms. All the hinges and doorknobs were black. The ceiling fans in the living room and the master bedroom were carved wood, shaped like propellers. The backsplash in the kitchen was a glass subway tile in a delicate pastel I still can't figure out. It might be seafoam, or pale mint, a blue-gray something. When I walked into the master suite, I think I actually lost my breath at the deep porcelain tub, the way the marble wrapped along the walls, the double vanity, all the glass. The whole house was perfect. I'd repaint it, change some fixtures, but everything else was exactly what I'd been looking for. The house had been on the market for months, difficult to sell because there were other houses the same size for much cheaper in the same neighborhood. What this house needed was someone who cared about shit like marble tiles and what color the hinges were. It had been waiting for me.

While the paperwork was being processed, I visited the house and named it: Shiny. The house for a god. It was a new construction, so no one had ever lived in it before, and it felt lonely. I would touch the walls and talk to it, walk through the rooms with my heart in my mouth, worrying that something would go wrong and we wouldn't end up together, this godhouse and me. On the first day of March, we closed, and when I walked into the house that afternoon, it felt different—because the house was **mine**.

I started work on it almost immediately and didn't stop for many weeks. We replaced light fixtures and wall plates, built garden boxes, carved glass inlays into the cabinet doors, and repainted all the walls with limewash, a specialty paint that has to be applied by hand with a brush, no rollers, no spraying. We went through gallons of it. We painted the tray ceilings gold and some of the bottom cabinets dark green. All of the furniture I ordered— the king bed, the massive dining table with marble feet, the velvet couches—had to be assembled on site. Everything was gold or brass, a deep green, a pale pink. I had never worked so hard to shape something into what I wanted it to look like. Sometimes, I curled up on the marble floor of my master closet and sobbed from exhaustion and sadness that I was doing this alone.

I couldn't share it with my family. Money had made things complicated—they would have told me I was being irresponsible, careless. Do you ever feel how familiar old stories can be when they're stitched onto you? When the people you loved are the ones doing the grafting? I wanted to see **myself,** not the version of me they store in their eyes. I wanted to settle into the house like a god, carve it the way I wanted, without human anxieties, fears, or limitations. I filled it with plants and art. It is more than a house, it's an entire dimension; you can feel it when you walk in. I stopped sending photographs because the house couldn't fit into them, just like it can't fit into this letter. It feels like a miracle.

Sometimes, when I walk through Shiny, I'm in shock at how much work I put into it, how customized it feels, how particular. I've never had a home in this country before, a place I wouldn't have to leave in a year or two. People keep talking about resale value, as if I'm going to sell it. I ignore them and grow a garden, full of chocolate habanero and purple bell peppers, red and orange and burgundy okro, deep violet sweet potatoes. The winter garden is coming along now, purple bok choy, dark nebula carrots, and ice-bred arugula.

I love this house so much, Marguerite. I love that I made it in my image, I love that it's mine. I'm even learning to love being alone in it—not sharing, allowing myself to stretch out into all of it. It used to feel too big, but I think I'm starting to fit.

When you come visit, can we plant shadow-beni in the garden? I would love that.

Nonexistent | Dear Ann

I am, to put it finely, dying.

It is interesting, how slow it is. Like offing the lights one room at a time, shuttering windows in slow motion. I am not sure how deep the dying will dig. Shiny is a tomb, a walled-off mausoleum. That is not a bad thing. It is probably a safe thing.

The thing about being hypervisible as a deviant body on the internet—which is really just a diluted version of the real deviant thing I am—is that it shows you how much the world does not want you to exist. It is peculiar, how targeted it becomes. It's not the specific strangers who matter, more so the majority they represent, the personal they represent: my family and the way they do not want me to exist as the thing I am, which means not wanting me to exist at all. I tell my therapist they do not see how I am bent backward to allow them in my life. She says, well, that position—bent and backward—is the one they think you belong in. So, of course, they do not see.

The thing about everyone wanting you not to exist is that it is very loud, but not even that, it's that I agree with them completely.

I, too, do not want to exist. We are of one deadly accord. I, too, do not think I belong in their ugly world, their violent world, keep suffering for what exactly? For more masks that strip the skin off my faces, again and again, day after day, the hungriest of masks?

So you want me to die. So I want to die. What do we do now? Will you come and kill me? What if I say please?

I deleted my social media. I've never done

that before; it has a different weight for me. I needed to kill some of my aspects. The therapist kept urging me to stand in my truth. I told her I would lose my family. She shrugged. It was not an inconsiderate shrug. It was a well, you remove who you have to remove. Stand in my truth? Does she know that means I must go mad? I must die?

Maybe the flesh will be spared if I just become a dead thing, the dead thing I already am, standing in that truth without the skinning masks of alive faces: pretending to be a child, a sister, a thing on the internet. I have become a freak on a pedestal for the Nigerians, aspiration on a screen, a lie of representation, a thousand lies angled on a camera. Standing in my truth means it all has to die. So I am dying.

Without the masks, there is so much pain. It might kill me in this reality, but that's par for the course. I write an angry letter to the magician, the god who doesn't let himself be a god, who corrupts himself with the weakness of the human mask he wears. I tell him I am writing it to be cruel, because he is the only soul close enough to mine who my hurt can hurt as much as it hurts me.

He does not reply. Days pass and he does not reply.

I see I am dead in more ways than I expected. It doesn't feel bad. Too many other things feel worse for that to feel bad. Humans are still traipsing through my grave. I cry every day. Yesterday, I burned my finger on hot brass. I locked myself in the closet and lay on the marble floor and cried. I am reading Oyeyemi's **The Opposite House.** Be careful with that book if you read it. It will drive you insane. It will destroy your masks.

I bury myself in Shiny. No one will find me if I die here. No one is coming to look for me. Nothing except a partnerspirit will ever feel like enough. I stop telling people about my hurt, because there is nothing you all can do for it—no one can save me. Everyone's hands have been chopped off; all they can do is wave their bleeding wrists at me sadly. Wave at the dying god. So many people hate me. That, too, is normal for a god, I suppose.

I will break everyone's heart. I can't help it.

I can't be what they want me to be. I can only be dead, and there is no one to come and die with me, play in the grave, go mad together.

Alone, I am suffocating. There is nothing more, really, to be done.

Thank you for reading this. I love you.

Dreams | Dear Katherine

The bar is outdoors, by the sea. It's dusk, and the beach is nothing more than the dark and hungry mouth of an ocean, in that way where all the sand is black, and the water is ink except for the bone-white break of surf. The waves sound like death. The people in the bar are terrified and silent. The man I'm waiting for is on the beach, pacing like a boast through the sand. I climb on one of the wooden tables while the owner of the bar looks over at me, his face creased in worry.

"I'm going to kill him," I tell the owner.

"If you want him alive, I suggest you get to him first."

He nods, concern spreading thickly around him. The man on the beach thinks of himself as bloodthirsty, thinks of the fight to come as one that belongs to him already. I look like a small woman. He is certain I can't hurt him. The owner, however, knows I'm a god—there's no bloodlust that can match mine. I'm considerate for allowing him the option of preventing a murder in his place of business, but the sentence still tastes true in my mouth.

I'm going to kill him.

I pace along the wooden tables and whistle, the tune echoing through the stretch of hungry air before me. I am swinging a weapon in my hand. It's an unidentifiable blur, but its weight is familiar and comfortable. The man on the beach waits for me to come to him. I want him to come to me instead, to walk his body into my waiting hands. I'm a little nervous, the way you get before something magnificent happens, adrenaline coursing through my flesh like arousal. I start singing: a ghost of a song, a dirge. Everyone in the bar is frozen, barely breathing from their fear. I'm used to that. It's how they should be, around me.

He's taking too long.

I taunt him aloud, calling him a coward who's afraid to face a woman. I'm not a woman, but that's not the point. It works—such strategy always works with men like these. He comes up the sand like a bull, snorting and enraged. The owner of the bar jumps into motion as well. I—the god—do not move. I only crouch slightly, grinning, heat in my hands, waiting for his flesh to arrive so that I can destroy it.

This is where the dream stops.

I startle awake with bloodthirst fresh under my tongue, my arms humming with excitement, rich with no fear, knowing I can't be killed. Power echoes through me like a song, but it begins to fade away even as the morning fades in. Reality feels like a sour disappointment, but I **remember,** Katherine. I remember how it felt, and I know it was true. Maybe not in this life or this dimension, but it was true, and I miss it so much.

Even in this reality, some of me believes I am invincible. I think of it as a vestigial godmemory, of having a body that was not this one, because this body is almost certainly fragile. Its bones would break under enough force; it would bleed, tear, rupture. It can't run very fast, or leap from building to building the way I do when asleep. I think I like that dream-self better. I've killed in that form before, many times. On a different beach, when cornered by men who were hunting me, I speared one of them through his kidney and the others dissolved. Another time, I felt the resistance of an ex-lover's throat under my knife, the dissatisfaction of the first stroke, the decision in the second. A line from my surgical training chastised me as his blood pumped over my hands: "Don't whittle," it said, "cut." I am always hunted in my dreams; no one ever catches me. I fly through air and run up walls when I am asleep; I have the body of a beast, another life lined with adrenaline and metal.

When I was younger, in this reality, I used to get into fights—quick hot things when I lost my temper. A classmate's braid ripped from her head, snaked inert on the girls' bathroom floor. A hand wrapping the throat of a college friend, a man much larger and stronger

than me, who'd had the temerity to unplug
my CD player when I specifically said not to.
I was sixteen. I forgot that I was flesh, that
the size of human bodies matters in a fight;
they don't matter if you're a god. I wasn't used
to being embodied. I fantasized about swinging cafeteria trays into people's teeth, scatter-
ing them across the floor of the dining hall. I
lay in bed and imagined being jumped in an
alley by humans who made their decisions on
premises that didn't apply to me. One, that
your victim will fight to save themselves, not
turn on you with a gleeful desire to kill. Two,
that your victim is afraid of dying. I imagined
the freedom such an attack would give me: to
kill someone with a good excuse, to couch it as
self-defense. I designed the godsmile I'd wear
on my face, just for them, for that private moment when they died and there was no one but
me watching their life seep into nothing, just
before I fell into careful human hysterics for
the benefit of arriving witnesses or authorities.
In these fantasies I was prepared to kill, and I
was prepared to die.

Precisely because of the irrationality of all
this, I don't fight anymore. I'm not prepared

for the way my humanity will disappoint my divinity. Dreams don't blur over into this particular reality; or perhaps I'm afraid that they will—that I'll lose my temper and revert to being a god on a bar table, mouth watering for blood. That when it's over, I'll wake up to human consequences, or that I won't wake up at all. Even in this paragraph, the worlds bleed over.

This is really all about power, the memory of it seeping through from the other side. Years ago, I dreamed I was the Messiah. It felt obvious, like a thing I had always known, a thing everyone else had somehow forgotten. It's one of my favorite stories; I think you'll like it.

I had an army. We were outside and it had just rained on the hill. I stood on an outcrop, cold grass under my bare feet, a thousand tired eyes watching me. I told them we all have a god in us. "I want you to know we all matter," I said, my voice ringing with preternatural clarity. They were mine, these loyal hearts waiting to stop beating for me. "We can be humans, or we can be flames," I called out. "We can burn, or we can **burn**!"

The sky was gray, and we'd fought so much already, but there was still more fighting to do. I was calm—I'm always calm before the killing. I wanted them to sing murder ballads, to carry holy edges, to be infected by the fire inside me—a licking yellow contagion that brushed them one by one, lighting up god after god, until all the terrible things we were about to do would be in worship of ourselves. I was, in retrospect, the only type of Messiah I could be.

I think about how all this could translate to this reality, this being flesh and dreaming of godselves. I wonder if the dreams are meant to be a blunt reminder of power. All my life, I've been hesitant to unfurl completely, worried that there won't be enough space for all of me, that I'm too much, too strange, too arrogant. I keep halfway secrets, like how failure isn't one of my fears; I'm only afraid of what I could become if I stopped being tentative, if I rooted myself instead in that dizzying sense of invincibility. This world is not particularly gentle with those whose volume defies decibels, but consider this. What if I faced it like a god waiting for a brawl on a bar table, like embodiment never weakened me? What would change? What could I accomplish?

The dreams translate power as violence— which makes sense for gods, even young embodied ones—but there are other possible choices. The absence of fear. The certainty of self. The ability to catalyze change in tired eyes clustered under a gray sky. The capacity to love past human sense. A knowledge of the future made firm because you're the one shaping it. Being free; all choices that seem desirable, colored only by the costs that come with them. There's no power without sacrifice, without losses, without a necessary insulation that can end up feeling indistinguishable from isolation. Embodied nonhumans are often terribly lonely.

Still, the other night, I severed three people's spines from their heads, pinning them to the wall like butterflies with a triangular spearhead. They were old and frail, dressed in rags; they died easily. Perhaps the dreams are a reassurance—that I can kill the parts of myself that are afraid, the human parts; that the distance between where I am and where

I could be, unfurled, is measured in just a few careful assassinations. Perhaps they are a reminder, a booster shot of power so I don't settle, a nudge that says while the life I want is built out of things I desire and fear in equal measure, blinding with monstrous possibility, it's still mine to hunt, to seize and drag home by the bloody throat, there for the taking.

If there's one thing I've learned from these dreams, it is, after all, how to take a life.

Consummation | Dear Kanninchen

Between the two of us, in this moment, we are several integrals' worth of madness.

Let's do it in a scatter, I suggest. Our clothes decide we are not meeting their emotional needs and so they break up with us, which is fine; we knew we would disappoint them anyway. Jumpsuits hold such grudges. The whole bed is an indigo airplane landing strip and I crash into it and fall two, three floors below, bounce off the building's foundations, ricochet back up into your arms with concrete wet in the corner of my eye. You catch me and your skin keeps rippling. There is no hard, there is no soft, there is five of you inside a square root of me; there is an eyeball rolling between keloided chest and remembering edema. There are precisely twenty-six and five-eighths exits located between both of our bodies. We take them all and eat the fleshdoors that held them.

I am preoccupied with the crevices of you, each tastes like a new language, you are such a teratoma. When I scream, you lost your hearing five weeks ago. When you come, I tasted it in my first kiss. I play games in riding you, grinding on just the head for half a lifetime, a slow slide down in our old age, and then we are reincarnated, and then I age us again, slamming all the way down. You are a torment in me, you now have a childhood with no sound, your hands trap me and rock; two fingers investigate us through a thin layer of cells and I am a seizure, sixteen of me is spilling on your hips.

It is important to you that I get to know myself and I believe in this, too, I think it is useful for our relationship, and learning it off your skin is, on the whole, an excellent method. Your body is a river in my palms;

eight thousand two hundred and fifty-three of you are looking down at me at the same time, and I have not known such joy as being stretched under a gaze like this. I am choked with emotion, you are thick with it, it deforms the anatomy of my face, my jaw, my gullet, a multiple truth. My forearms have decided that (a) they are chains, (b) they are lonely, and (c) they are shy, so they lock in my back and leave the maneuvering to lips and tongue. The tonsils claim to help but we all know they don't do anything, lazy bastards.

I am an adventure book with a strangled siren for a spine, I am a muffled beat. You are a wrap behind my skull, a shout of flesh knotted in my hair, a desperate and dying piston. There is a tremendous emptying even before the emptying and I keep my eyes open to see it and you keep your eyes open to show me, and all our spikes and scales and scarlet and batleather bits snap into focus and my talons are in your hamstrings and your wings are quivering, breaking down the brick of the walls, and your eyelids shift to the corners of your eyes but you don't close them because you are showing me, and my irises are turmeric and

I see you and the sound that tears out from your throat as you come in mine is dark purple and it slithers down your body as you shudder. Time decides to stretch, the sound slides down the saliva on my chin and slips down my body to where my fingers are molding gold, and you don't understand, that sound is a beast I would worship, so when it touches me, it drags a counterpart up into my mouth, time reverts, our sounds and small deaths are synced, vocal cords sending vibrations around you. You are filled with aftershocks, you do not let go of my head, we are buried like this.

They never figure out what to put on our joint headstone.

Home | Dear Jahra

The last time I saw you, you'd been stranded in Los Angeles for ten hours. Ann lives there, and I was flying in to see her, but you didn't know any of this until I hit you up and got into a shuttle to find you after I landed. When you ran across the terminal to hug me, you looked just like you did in New York: a god in flesh-colored garments, with a body trained for channeling, trained for the kinds of magic I wish I could perform. You were taller than I remembered. You held me so tightly and it felt like my skin didn't fit, because you were holding me and this skin felt clumsy between two gods. I can't remember what snacks I had: sweet potatoes, a guava, something that I fed you with. I called Ann and she swung by from work and picked us up and we went to a terrible little restaurant and sat at a table together. Three nonhumans together in the same physical space is a force that weights the world in the place we are gathered. The only other time I've seen it happen was when you and I and Eloghosa ate burgers in New York, and I think we were shy then. I wonder what it would be like with four of us, five, six, eighty-seven thousand of us.

Los Angeles brings out my godmode—which is just a thing about remembering, not a thing about being. I can breathe and my lungs draw power in. I am not even remotely afraid. I am a deity in hotel rooms. The three of us ordered soup at the terrible little restaurant and talked about home and belonging and what it was like to claim ontologies that we might not be accepted in. I cried when you told me about that museum, about the walls that folded open in its vaults, and the entities they had locked away in there, wrongly, too close. We've been hunting for homes and I think it's been hard to see that so much of it is threaded inside us already. We're drawing maps, back to our villages, back to our languages. If I remember correctly, you've been learning Fijian lately and unlocking doors with the back of your throat. How does it feel? I gave up some of that journey because I realized that I'm making work too fast and too hungrily to carve out time for perfecting another language. I do know the power in it, though. I only speak Igbo when I talk to Ala and my chi. I don't have a country of vocabulary, but I learn enough, clawing my jaw through it because it's worth it to speak to them with this tongue.

After I decided to write **Freshwater,** I knew I had to go home and complete something. I wasn't sure quite what. There's a river in Anambra State called Idemmili, which is also the name of the god who lives in the river. She comes on land as a python, curls herself around the children who live on her banks and sleeps in their beds. I knew I was following a python, so I thought I had to go there and find a priest of Idemmili. I don't know how I was so blind, looking in all the wrong places. Every attempt I made to organize a trip back home for that failed. I wanted someone else to anoint me, to mark my forehead with ash or blood or clay and tell me I was right, that my divination of myself was accurate. Everyone else seemed to have a babalawo, a padrino, a tío, someone who would guide them. There are some roads you don't want to have to walk alone, but I've never been allowed to touch my hand to another entity's feet.

I remember when a former partner took me to see their babalawo—how the rage simmered inside my chest, hot with contempt that wasn't mine, itching under my skin, wanting to be away from there and the wrongness of that world. The babalawo told my former partner what sacrifices would have to be made for our relationship to succeed, then laughed and said the sacrifices would never happen. **You're fucking right,** a voice in my head hissed back. I kept quiet. My former partner got angry when I told them I wouldn't do any of it: no knife slicing across the feathered neck, no blood slipping into the sand. After I broke up with them, they found me dancing on my birthday with a new lover and gave me a bag full of things: scraps of fabric, a letter. I threw it in a trash can on a street corner, because they were all cheap spells and I am my deity-mother's child. Do you have stories of how people tried shit with you like you're not who you are?

I tried to go to Ile-Ife. I tried to go to a Yemaya ceremony on a beach in Trinidad. I could feel the roads closing in the air, the stench of **you are not allowed** thick and thrumming. I don't remember how, but I figured out that I wasn't meant to go to the Idemmili River because I had no business there. My python wasn't the one from the water, it was the one from the land—Ala's avatar. So I figured I had to go home and find one of Ala's shrines, talk to a priest or something, tell them what I was, who I was. I wondered if they would recognize me, if they'd feel it in the red earth under all our feet, or if they'd just see someone with no language, with tattooed skin and a Western contamination in their voice, with a face and hair that betrayed outside blood. I know you know how that feels. I worried that they'd laugh and send me away, and what would I do then? These claims I was making were not small things, to call Ala mother when she's the most powerful deity to my people, you know?

In Brooklyn, over tea, I talked with Zina Saro-Wiwa about what makes a folktale a folktale, how it can break timelines, how it is defined, how in the end it is just a story in this form told by a person from this culture. Zina told me about Ogoni masquerades she was making to be worn by women, since the men claimed that no woman could carry a spirit, which is of course bullshit. She asked me why I felt I needed permission from the priests, and you know, Jahra, I didn't have an answer. I thought that was just the next step in the journey I was on, getting that blessing.

Blood purity in doing the work we do is such a thing. I wish I saw more people talking about it. We worry so much, we question ourselves, as if we have less of a birthright because so many humans have told us we do. I let all of that go when I accepted not being human: blood is only a flesh thing, and there's no way that humans would be the ones with the authority to "authenticate" me. Gods don't give a fuck about what outside bloodlines run through these bodies; we belong to them so utterly either way.

So, then, I had to ask myself: If it wasn't necessary to get permission from the priests, why was I going home? What was I going home for if I accepted that my birthright was the only authority I needed to move in? I don't know if this happens for you, but most of the time my prayers are answered by a knowing I have no way of knowing, a ray of clarity piercing my mind, a thing that no one has whispered but that I know is true. As soon as I asked, the answer showed up. **Go home to greet Ala.** That was it, stunning and simple, go home and pay your respects to your deitymother. The road unfurled like a red tongue in my eye.

I bought the ticket home, and this time I was allowed to return. I flew to Lagos, and then to Owerri, and my human father came to collect me. As we drove back to Aba, I looked out of the window at the land leaping by, the waist-high grass a cool and fast green. **Nne,** I told her in Igbo. **I have come home. I have come to greet you. Please, open the road for me.**

A thousand snakes appeared in the grass, translucent in my mind, swimming through the green like it was water, leaping in bends along the car. Escorts, avatars of her. Welcome home. You are not alone. I exhaled, knowing she had received me. I only had four days to find my way to one of her shrines, and I had no idea how I was going to do it, but I wasn't worried. The road was always hers to open, not mine. My job was to show up.

The next morning, my human father told me we had to go next door to say hello to his neighbor. I didn't want to. This neighbor wasn't the man who had lived there when I grew up and thank God for that. The old neighbor had groped me when I was twelve; he called my little sister his wife because it was his car that took her to the hospital when she was run over at six. When I started avoiding him, after that day he cornered me in his parlor, everyone scolded me. I was pleased when he died. I didn't particularly want to go back into that parlor again, no matter who was living in it now, but my human father is stubborn and insists on propriety, on showing off his foreign-based children, his prides who rarely come home. We went next door.

The new neighbor was a redhead, with skin like a road in the village. He asked what brought me home; I told him it was research for a book I was writing—half a lie, cobbled together with truth. He kept asking for details and I kept stalling because I didn't want to talk to him about my deitymother. He was a complete stranger; why would I tell him about Ala? I kept her in my chest, scales pressing against my inside flesh, filling me up. He kept asking and I could see my human father getting impatient with my reticence, so I told the red neighbor that I was looking for a shrine of Ala, but I didn't know where to find one.

He laughed. "Ala is everywhere," he said. "I can help you." I heard that line quite a bit: Ala is everywhere. It's so literal because she's the earth, but also because she's a deity that's ubiquitous across Igboland, she's not restricted to region like Idemmili is, so there isn't just one central shrine to her. Ala's shrines are, like her, everywhere. When the red neighbor made his offer, my human father bristled. I'm not sure if it was because we were talking about a deity, or if it was because another man was giving his child something he couldn't. He can be proud like that. He started blustering about how it was unnecessary, but the red neighbor ignored him, which surprised me. I expected him to defer to my father because I was his child; if he didn't want me traipsing into the village looking for a shrine, the protocol would be to comply with his wishes. Instead, the red neighbor got on his phone and called a man in Umuahia who could take me to the shrine. In that moment, I realized that the road was opening. I had fought coming to the house, fought telling him what I needed, but now that I'd surrendered, two days into my stay, here was the path slashing its way into existence right in front of me. I had prayed and my deitymother was answering.

The red neighbor's connect in Umuahia said that it would be too much for him to come all the way to Aba to pick me up and take me to the shrine and back. By then, however, my human father had surrendered to the excursion. What else is there to do when faced with the will of a deity who is bringing her child home? You bend, you bow, even if you have no idea what your spine is doing.

The next day, a pastor friend of my father's arrived to take me to Umuahia. Perhaps, to them both, it felt like protection for what I was doing. We got on the bus on Aba-Owerri Road and sat in front, next to the driver. The pastor began an impassioned prayer over the vehicle and our journey, and the passengers welcomed it with amens. I could feel the prayer, hot and fervent, pouring like itchy syrup over my skin; disgust beat at the back of my throat. Be quiet, I told myself, let him do his nonsense. The road can't be closed, it's already too late. I could feel Yshwa's amusement and it irked me. "You know he's talking to you," I muttered in my head.

"I know he thinks he's talking to me," Yshwa replied. "They're so loud, aren't they?" I didn't answer.

They are hypocrites; I know exactly the kind of bile that this pastor and even my human father would summon up if they knew even half of what I am. Maybe some people forget, but I don't. Did I ever tell you about the first time I came home after I disclosed I was queer? I was dressing more masculine then, with my chest bound and my hair cut short. I refused to go to the town I was raised in because I didn't know if my human father would let me leave. Everyone told me I was being irrational, but I remember the man who raised me; I remember his face as he beat my sister in the corridor of our home, her small body cringing and crying as he hit her over and over, holding on to one of her skinny arms so she couldn't run away. When he came to see me in Lagos, he asked if the friend I was staying with knew I was gay. I told him she did and my human father looked at me as his voice curled. "How does she **tolerate** you?" he asked, disgust sliming over his tongue.

Fuck these Christians, is my point.

Once we made it to the village, we met the man who was our contact, and he took us to a large compound. The owner had died, he explained, and it was his wife left. They were worshippers, and shrines marked the large yard. A goat was tied and bleating in one corner. When the woman came out, I was shocked to see how small and bent she was, how meek her movements were. I had expected a different kind of authority—but what do I know about being a widowed practitioner in a place like home, with men being the way they are? She led us into her parlor and the two men who brought me there started explaining why we'd come. "We're not here for any fetish thing," they kept saying, and I had to bite back a smile. She nodded, and then I realized everyone was waiting for me to start asking questions. The room snapped around me, cornering me. I needed to talk to her alone; I couldn't say anything in front of these men.

"Can you show me some of the shrines?" I asked, calculating as quickly as I could. I knew the men would be too scared to come with us, and I was right. They flinched as she agreed, and I followed her out into the compound. She explained to me that there would be one shrine to Ala close to the house, and a main one in the forest. We stood by the home shrine and I explained to her why I had

come. I told her what my name was, what had
pulled me, how Ala spoke to me. She nodded and listened, impassive, as I spoke, and
I started to wonder how much of her expres-
sion was a mask, which skins she was wearing
around strangers. I asked if we could go see
the main shrine and she said yes. As we headed
out of the compound, she waved to a man in
another house. "Bia," she called out. "Anyi.
na-aga ịhụ Ala!" He got up and jogged over
to us and I hid a smile. The way she said it
was so casual. **Come. We're going to see Ala.**
She made it sound like we were dropping by a
neighbor's house.

I still remember that walk into the forest.
Ala's practitioner was wearing a synthetic red
wig; the ground beneath our feet was red,
too. Green vegetation rose around us past our
shoulders and the sky was a shocking blue. I
took a picture of it in my mind; I wanted to
remember precisely this moment, if nothing
else. What does your village look like? I saw
my deitymother in mine, by a gorge in the
earth, and I told the woman which village I
was from, where I was born. We spoke for a

little while as other villagers walked through
the forest and exchanged greetings as they
passed us.

When it was time to head back to the compound, I turned around and behind me, I
heard her say softly to the man, "Nke a dị ike."
This one is powerful.

Before we stepped back into her house, I
made quiet arrangements for an offering to
Ala, and took the woman's phone number.
The pastor and contact were waiting for us
in the parlor, and they insisted on praying
over her, calling on Jesus more times than I
thought was polite, but she sat with her eyes
closed and said amen with a fervor that even I
couldn't imitate.

Back at my human father's clinic, the pastor exulted over how the day had gone. "God
opened the way for us," he said. "We encoun-
tered no problems! I am sure that our purpose
was to speak about Jesus to that woman." I
remember marveling at his version of the story.
These four men—my father, the red neighbor,
the pastor, the contact—they had all been
moved by my deitymother, pawns in a mission
they were completely unaware of, thinking

they were serving their God when really they were carrying out Ala's will. The contact had kicked up a fuss when it was time to pay him, emphasizing over and over again that he wouldn't usually do anything like this, he was a Christian, he didn't like these fetish things.

I thought, What else could my mother do for me if I asked? Who else could she move, so smoothly that they would have no idea they were even being used?

That's how I went home. It would have been rude for me to doubt who or what I was after that, but I didn't share this story publicly for a long time. I didn't need to tell it to validate who I was to the humans; those who saw me for what I am didn't need this to believe me, and those who didn't believe me wouldn't believe me even if Ala manifested out of thin air and wrapped her scales around me in front of their own eyes. My point is: This is between us and the gods, not between us and the humans. The gods are always clear with us, they are the ones we need to listen to. Recently, I've been thinking about these earthly homes less as homes and more as places of origin for our embodied forms.

After our dinner in LA, when we were leaving the restaurant, Ann and I walked behind you on our way out. "She walks like a god," Ann said to me, and it made me smile because you really fucking do. It's magnificent, how you carve through the air. I hope you find all the homes you're looking for.

Desire | Dear Eugene

I've been dreaming about you, lucid storytellings, fantasies that fill the space between sunrise and the real of the world crashing in. We're in an elevator, a hotel somewhere, mirrors and gold wrapping the walls. I want, almost desperately, to touch your skin, to have you touch mine. In this dream, you want the same thing.

We are flirting with the air around each other, taut circles that grow tighter and tighter, closer and closer. Your breath is against my neck, my heartbeat is a mountain falling in my ears. The elevator pings floor after floor, time runs out of air, and one of us, it doesn't matter who, says we shouldn't. One of us, it doesn't matter who, is lying. Your hand floats at the flash of skin between my shirt and the waistband of the joggers I'm wearing. It's not a deliberate thing, this floating, more like the skin next to my navel called quietly and you couldn't help but answer, and once there it's so easy to slide past the waistband, to push into the slate-gray cotton underneath, and just so, your fingers slip and you hiss a breath into my ear.

"Goddamn," you whisper, "you're so fuck-ing wet."

The elevator chimes a warning a beat before the doors open and we pull apart. This game doesn't get old for some of me—inject the for-bidden, the wrong, the **my god, how I want everything I shouldn't** directly into my veins. The dream splinters and breaks into pieces. I spin them around in my head and catch the light. The pause at my hotel room door where you decide who you're going to be right now. The glimmer on your fingertips. The hunger stalking behind your eyes, eroding thought, the way it drags your eyelids down and softens your mouth. I think this is one of my favorite pivots—there's such loud potential for bliss if you fall just the right way. In this dream, you step in, the door closes, you kiss me like it's worth damnation.

We pull off shirts, fabric licking skin, hands and heat underneath. In this dream you are deliciously selfish, you are here with me, we have burned the rest of the world away, we are reckless and starving and greedy. In this dream, you want me back. Your arms hold up your shoulders as you look down at me, your hair falling in my face, mine in your fist, the duvet a displaced cloud as our combined weight presses into the bed. In this dream, you are hard and suffering the best kind of agony, we are impatient and there will be time for slow exploring later, but for now it's just you entering me and time moaning into nothing, into a blind and near-religious ecstasy. You bite my shoulder, your beard scraping my skin as you sink entirely into me, and I wonder what it feels like for you, to make a god whimper with pleasure.

I like this story and its variations, fantasies

spun out of salt and sugar. They are entertaining dimensions to slip into. You in my bed, your mouth on me, mine on you. We are always so hungry, even when we start off slow. I've spun this world so powerfully in my head, it takes me a moment to remember it's not real. That you're walking around in the flesh somewhere, making love to your partner, living a completely unrelated life. I know this isn't really about you, this is about the beast of my wants, and you are beautiful and gentle enough that it's easy to play a game and cast you in my dreams. I wonder if this is creepy. I have to be careful. I make worlds and they don't always merge well with the one everyone else is living in; they can be safer apart, but I'm also the type of troublemaker who bends a world real just so I can live in it for a bit. That's a pretty way of saying I'd fuck you in real life—the dreams might not be true, but the desire is, stabled and fat on stories.

I don't know if you'd want me outside the dream. I've wanted people who wanted me but wouldn't act on it. I've wanted people who made fun of my want, called me thirsty to my face because I was supposed to be more modest, let them be the ones who fed on me. But I'm starving, this world never seems to give me enough of anything. I want to squeeze existence until it runs a bloody pulp down my arms, wet and yielding. Give me everything, give me your flesh, your offerings, the salt of your neck, the break in your voice, your body, your words, your time, your conscience, your loyalties, your whole and beating heart. Cut a lamb open in my bed and let it bleed out restraint and common sense, set it on fire, find a new discipline in me.

All my worshippers flee at some point.

I talked to your play brother about you, not to ask his permission, but to be honest. I think that's a lot of what love is. I used to be married, you know. We got divorced years ago, not long after I described myself to my friends and family as queer. It didn't go well; several of them assumed I had lied to my husband, tricked him into marrying me. When I started dating after the divorce, I couldn't believe how much people lied to each other. My ex-husband used to be my best friend; back in college, he was the first person I told when I liked a girl. He sent me off to queer play parties after we moved to Brooklyn and listened to me tell him about the people I kissed there. I thought love was always honest; I didn't know how other people moved. So of course, I told your play brother about this desire for you, the same way I told him about the last man I slept with— a tall stranger I met in a salsa club in London while on tour. I took the stranger back to my hotel; the room was washed in red by a light under the armchair. We showered and I didn't have any lotion, so we used coconut oil afterward. It was the Blackest thing ever, I said, us rubbing it into each other's skin, and we laughed. Sampha's album played on loop as we fucked gently and talked about our divorces. I signed a copy of my book for him and I never saw him again.

Your play brother knows all these details, because I think a lot of what love is, is just telling the truth. Also, he asked. I don't think he'd ask about you, and I don't think I'd tell if this dream came true. It's different when you two know each other.

I didn't grow up with this kind of desire; I wonder what it was like for you. I had curiosity, sure, but not desire, not even when I was a teenager. If you read **Freshwater,** then you know about the boy who put his hands on me and did things to my body—not the one when I was a child in Aba, the other one, when I was a kid in college—and you know about the splintering that caused, about my other selves who arrived in the bloody wake of that. For a long time, I wasn't there when desire kicked in; the other me was. It took me years to show up in my own body and balance out all of my selves. I learned how to soften some of the edge; I learned that it was okay to be tender and touch someone with a weight of softness in your hand. I let myself and the vines of the other me twist around each other—not quite forming one thing, but I'm not a singular being, so that's okay, it makes sense.

This might not be particularly sexy, but it's not meant to be.

My point is: I was a sweet kid, they did violent things to me, and I've become a planet since then. I'll always be that sweet kid, but now my spirit is also a pulse of shock waves, a terrible force in the old-school sense of **terrible,** like what an angel actually is versus what we reduced them to. A small god with the desire to match, with a dial that breaks past the painted numbers, always looking for someone to play with—not to toy with, but to match me, to not be afraid, not flinch from the way I look at them, not try to crush me with their palms and elbows and words, make me into something less brilliant, something that won't hurt their eyes as much.

It's why I spin these dreams, cast people like you in them. You seem like you have tenderness wired into your body, by choice. Like you might be able to play a little with me, maybe not for long, but for a pocket of time. It's make-believe, I know, but imagination is what I deal in. I think I would be safe with you. I don't think you would hurt me. That's important to me now; I got tired of playing with men who had cruelty just a slip behind their eyes. Your play brother got me hooked on gentle. If you want to know what he said when I told him I wanted you, ask him. You know he won't lie to you. Neither will I.

This letter is full of secrets, though. Some of them are poorly kept, like how I'm attracted to unavailable people because their outcomes are consistent, the prophecies are kept steady

in my mouth, coming true even as I cry over
them. There's no lonely like a god's lonely.
All my worshippers flee at some point. Other
secrets are softer, tucked deeper. Like how I
don't actually want this dream to come true,
not like this.

I don't want to fuck you in a suspended
moment that will crash, spiraling smoke, into
guilt. I don't want you to feel bad afterward,
like you betrayed someone. I don't want you
to betray someone. The thing about desire is
that I want you to choose it, freely and safely,
on a sure wing. That face, the one of the other
me, brash and bold, it has been a useful one.
There's another face, the one your play brother
told you about, the one he sees when he calls
me the softest person he knows. The one where
I wouldn't write this letter if I thought casting
either of us in this dream would betray him;
the one where I ran it by him, not for permission, but because I want to be gentle with
the people I love—and that means telling the
truth. Even about the desire to love someone
else, even just for a little while, a moment on
a mountain, a ram's blood allowing us to live
without guilt. I don't think feeling this desire

is wrong. I wonder if it thrilled through you, if it confused you because I'm not a woman, if you pressed it flat and stole its breath because you're taken and you're loyal to your boys and he was right there the whole time. He chose something else, though, not me. I wonder if he talked to you about it. I think he chose himself, in the best way, in the put on your own oxygen mask first save your life way, but I wonder if he told you how it broke both our hearts, mine at the very least to utter pieces.

There is a woman I assume you love, someone real, not made of dreamskin. Or maybe she is made of dreamskin, the kind that has come true. I want to say you wouldn't betray her, but I don't know you like that. I know men, I know their unscrupulous hungers better. I wonder where the difference between hunger and desire falls, if it folds into consumption, if one is more desperate than the other, more unthinking. In this dream, there is no time for thought, because thought is a cock-blocker. There is no time for the past, for reconstructed memories of her hands on you or his on me, there is only the blinding wash of want, the void it creates, the costs you will pay to fill it. That's always the trick, isn't it? To burn the outside world, to make it unreal, to create a bubble where there are no consequences for the things we did in hunger. But, like I said, I don't want what follows, when we wake up in ashes, smelling of smoke. What if you can't quite look at me? Like I became a terrible, blinding thing, reflecting an interior you pretended you didn't have. No one asked you to lie to yourself.

I want too much, I know. I want everything. Bubbles that last forever. My hunger fed with no cost. Dreams to come true. Someone to want me as much as I want them. Someone who will act on it. The smoke of a thousand burnt offerings drying my tears. A worshipper who stays until their death or mine. In this dream, I make you understand what it feels like to be worshipped, even just for a moment on a mountain.

I wonder if we'll talk about this letter in real life, outside these pages, outside this world I bent into being. In my time away from writing this, I think perhaps I'm exaggerating—maybe this was just a brief crush, a fleeting want. But then you drop me a line or I see your face and the desire roars awake again, consistent and hungry. Take me back, touch me again. In this dream my doorbell rings, and when I open it you're standing there, tired and wearing black like you always do, but you smile when you see me. You drop your things, the door closes, and you kiss me like it's worth salvation, and in that moment, my god, it really is, isn't it?

I'm saying this like you'll remember, like you were there. Go get some sleep.

It's just a dream.

Holy | Dear Eloghosa

think there's something wrong with me.

I feel like a toy in a glass box. Like no one wants to spend their real life with me, love on me till I become dog-eared, ripped at the seams from undying clots of affection. I don't understand why the people I want don't want me—and I mean all of me, the parts that can't unlook things, the parts without lies. Anything less than that is not want; it's incomplete, it's conditional desire, alive only as long as everything stays easy. Superficial. When I say want, I mean showing up. I mean the kind of love that asks you every morning to be better; I mean saying yes to it every day, no matter how hard it feels. I would be so good, I would try my best, but no one wants me in their world. I don't even mean in the hand-inside-chest way, but just sharing a home together or a thousand other possible things: flying to Vietnam and renting a house, staying in separate wings most of the time and making work; going to Sri Lanka again; doing quiet road trips in the desert, up a wooded coast. I'd take anything, but people only want to play with me sometimes, and then they put me back in the glass box and go back to their other lives, with the people who aren't as terrifying as me, who don't ask as much of them, who don't expect them to make and bend and burn through worlds. The women they keep saying they're unhappy with, but who will fuck them with misery seething under their beds and bear their children.

You and I know that there are millions of people who are easier than we are. In the dark of night, my demons don't tell me I'm worthless. They tell me I am too powerful, that no one will ever want me for it, that I don't deserve love or happy endings because I chose too much, I ate too much of the world, I refused to starve and as punishment, I will be starved.

I feel like an indulgence, a royal prisoner in a tower room, the one they dream with, their mouths on my skin as if my sweat is a drug and something in me is, isn't it? Something in me is bright and brilliant enough that they want to plug their hands into it, like there's a gash of blood and water in my side and they're pushing their fingers into it, lances of flesh, vinegar dripping from my mouth. They bleed me of dreams, spinning worlds that float across my ceiling, and I am a fool, a little fool, never realizing until it's too late that these dreams are just games to them. They are all very real to me; I would have made them all real. I would be so good; I would try my best. There is something bright and brilliant in me. It doesn't make me feel special. It makes me terribly alone.

When they have played and dreamed and fucked enough—it usually takes two years, they can't sustain illusions longer than that— they climb off my bed and put their pants on,

tucking themselves in and zippering themselves up. They say things about what is impossible, what they cannot do, and leave me
sobbing because I thought we were going to
take the world and pour it behind our teeth,
down our throats. I thought I wouldn't be
left alone. They step out of the tower room,
through the glass they'll never admit exists;
they leave, and leave me alone. I am not real.
It doesn't matter what you do to something
that isn't real.

I know how to make the glass box pretty. I
made it into a planet of a snow globe; I belong
only in the worlds I create. My doctors say to
give myself the things other people can't, build
a home no one wants to share with me, carve a
life no one wants to walk next to me in. I wonder if they see how a place this alone is a cage,
an isolation tent, quarantined godquarters.
Everyone else gets to take off the hazmat suits
and go back to their lives. No one wants to live
with me. There's a song by Massive Attack by
that name, "Live with Me"; I used to listen to
it on loop, imagining that someone who loved
me was finally, finally saying these things to
me. No one ever has.

I don't know what I did to make people un-want me so.

My therapist reminds me that it can't all be stories of what people did to me—that I was there, that I made choices, too. She's right. I have chosen many things over being alone, things that were bad for me. Maybe I thought that was all I was worth. I think of dreams as drugs, myself as a drug, the reality shimmering around me as a high. I think about how they pretend that dreaming so carelessly with me isn't violent, just because it feels so good to them. Bind tight rubber around your arm, push me into the crook of your elbow, and I stop becoming a person. I stop becoming something you can hurt. I am entirely a rush, an escape, and no one ever thinks that ecstasy has feelings of its own. Or, maybe they just don't give a fuck. Nothing matters more than how we make them feel, right? Why did I **stay**?

In my last letter to you, I talked about unfurlings. I talked about becoming as big as we are, fuck the consequences. There are so many ways to be unseen. If we are as addictive as we are now, how much more desirable will we become as we expand? I don't mean desirable in a good way, but rather, that devotion they ply us with, that attention that feels like it could be love, those arms reaching toward and through us in a flood of supplication, asking: Give us light, make us feel like we are gods, too, see the things in us that no one else believes in, make us believe they are real, see us, see the best of us, it is only in your light that we become holy. They are hungry and we are infinities of faith. I don't know if we can stop giving, but maybe we should try. No one is going to abstain from us on their own. I do know that their hunger hurts us, and they don't see any of this because everyone forgets that even the sun will die one day. It is dangerous to advertise the kind of power we have.

I didn't even realize how much of it I was masking until I bought and bent the godhouse down in the swamp. When I threw myself into customizing it, that distracted me from how much of a beast the house was. It was brand new then, a blinding white with haint-blue touches, floor-to-ceiling marble, warm light flooding through south and west windows; it was intimidating even before I put my hands

on it. Once I did, it flexed even harder: gold
ceilings and fixtures, acacia wood and velvet
couches, limewashed walls. Everyone who
came there looked at the godhouse and then
looked at me and asked what I did. How can
you afford this, they meant, just you alone? I
was overwhelmed.

The godhouse made me visible to strangers I would've hid from otherwise; I couldn't
pretend I was this little harmless person. They
looked at the godhouse and they saw money,
which meant power, amplified by me being
a storyteller, because what kind of storyteller
did you have to be to own a place like this. I
was terrified. The house felt too big for me; it
felt wrong, like I should have bought it years
into my career, not thirteen months after
my first book. For weeks, I didn't sleep well
there, worried that God would punish me for
being so bold, for bending the world like this.
It was Ann who talked me down, who told
me that the house was oversized precisely so I
could grow into it, so I could have the space
to learn how to unfurl. I needed that much
room, as vast as it felt. We never understand
how vast we are. We may spend the rest of our

lives finding out that we have no borders, no boundaries, pushing into greater sizes, being both terrified and delighted when we discover that there's nothing there to stop us. I thought it was disrespectful to God that I was trying to live like a small god, fragments of teachings about humility and destroying the ego still fluttering around in my head. Ann laughed and asked me to consider the possibility of a God delighted at the idea of us trying to live like one, a fond and indulging God. That concept shifted so much for me and I have been tentatively allowing myself to be more and more daring, allowing that God is not punishing me for being as radiant as I was made to be, that I am, in fact, being obedient by living like this. So. I am ablaze and so is my world, so is my godhouse, so is my work. So is my heart, so are my hands when they touch the supplicant's skin, so is my faith washing over them like a baptism. I burn so well that I don't burn at all.

I confess, I have used this fire to call people to me. It's not difficult; so many of them are cold and hungry, and we know how to feed them a world they can't build when they're by themselves. But I stopped, I swear I did. Summonings like that come with costs: you can "get" anyone you want, sure, but it won't take long before you realize it's not enough, or it doesn't taste like you thought it would, and you're left with a hunger they could never have enough meat for. I stopped, I tried to mind my own business, but a god on fire is a god on fire, so don't think people won't hunt it down.

I still haven't figured out what balance could look like, how to cope with the way they curl away when I reach out—either because I put too much weight in a step the humans keep light, or because everyone else is playing a game I have no patience for, a coy dance of lies and masks, mapped out with inaccurate criteria for power. It feels almost impossible to connect with people, and I watch other people do it like it's nothing, like it's the easiest instinct in their bellies. It is wrenching for me; it takes stupendous amounts of effort, and it rarely goes well. I am not like the others; I cannot spread myself out in the open and take my chances.

Ann was the one who taught me that the word **holy** means to be set apart for a specific purpose. I remember, back when I started writing **Freshwater,** how my lovers were removed, one by one. I was furious, lonely and longing, and not allowed. The stricture was loud and clear, like God's hand heavy and warning on my shoulder. I tried to ignore it; this had been one of my few small comforts through embodiment, how could it be taken away from me? I didn't last very long. My body itself started to shut down, screaming in pain whenever my remaining lover tried to penetrate it. Eventually I just curled up in agony, laughing to myself at how brutal these instructions were. Soon, he was removed from my life completely.

Part of me wishes I could explain to them that it wasn't personal, there are so many things I would have kept doing if God hadn't stopped me by force.

Does anyone talk about how heartbreaking it is to be set apart? It doesn't make me feel special. Or rather, I was raised being told I was special, so there's nothing particularly special about that by now, you know? Special is a baseline. Special doesn't always mean good things. It means you stand out; the rules may be bent for you somewhere, but they will be hammered harder against you somewhere else. Special can mean horrors that no one else will see or understand or believe. They say terrible things are done in darkness, but terrible things are also done in a light too blinding for anyone else to look at directly. Special can mean being an idol no one thinks can bleed, and even if you do, it doesn't mean what it does for everyone else, it is a marvel, a thing to pray at, a thing to touch with reverence. No one really hears your screams if they are divine, you precious breathing relic.

Holy means your life is not yours. You are being wielded by something else, and I think it's supposed to make us feel better that we are handled by God, but sometimes it doesn't feel like enough. It feels like voids yawning through, dazzling with pain. It feels like madness and a cage made of iridescent glass. It feels like a century of reincarnated hearts breaking at the same time.

I don't want to be alone. I would give up the rest of the world willingly if I was granted select respites. I would ask for a small circle of holy lovers, luminous dreamers with no need for my fire because they are burning just as much as I am, even just one, that we may be immolated in each other's arms. Holy means you surrender to a will that is greater than yours. I kneel in the glass box as blood and water pour from my side. I pray not to be forsaken.

There is no lonely like a god's lonely.

Anointing | Dear Ann

We could solve so many problems if we just went mad. I mean all the way mad, so lost that it never occurs to us to even think about how other people see us, what ripples we're casting in our families, what hostility we will provoke by showing our true faces. When we push forward with power, other things push back. I wonder if madness would function as a shield.

It would certainly be easier if we didn't know who we are, what we are—if we were the kind of entities who let other people describe and

define us, if we lived inside the lines spool-
ing out of their mouths. People want to be the
ones drawing the lines, building the boxes,
making the names. Maybe because stories live
inside all those structures, and if you're the
one controlling the stories, then you're the one
in power. So they get really angry when you
name yourself, especially if you're the type of
thing they were expecting to name. You know
how it works: they form a circle around you,
point, and call you a name you're supposed to
flinch from, a name you're supposed to deny
and be afraid of. That way, their naming becomes a weapon and what you are becomes a
shame, a sentence, a tire around your neck rich
with fire. Witch. Demon. Ọgbanje. When you
name yourself, however, you take the power
from the wet, foaming flesh of their mouths
and mold it in your hand as if it's nothing,
swallow waiting to slide down your throat,
slickened with the soup of your self-knowing.

I thought about this a lot with **Freshwater**—
what it meant, first of all, to publicly name
myself ọgbanje. Being one used to be a secret, something to hide from the humans, because once they found out they always tried to

destroy the iyi-ụwa and lock the ọgbanje into
flesh. But culture is not static, and we are decades away from that world, so I can afford
to be bold and open. What are they going to
do? Which human is going to force me to a
dịbịa? You can't find my iyi-ụwa, it's dissemi-
nated in my flesh. Did the humans think
that time would move forward for only them?
Everything advances, mutates, we are in new
worlds constantly.

I knew that other Nigerians would call me
a liar, claim I was making it all up as a publicity stunt, something white people would find
interesting. You know how our people are. To
self-name as an entity breaks the rules, because
then it means we've taken the naming and
storytelling power, to wield it for ourselves.
It's arrogant on their part—how does it make
sense that only humans would have the authority to identify and name nonhumans, that
we're not allowed to name ourselves? Some of
it is because they see themselves as the center,
with the unquestionable right to define what is
other. The magician once said it was an effect
of colonialism—this interest in taxonomy, a
white man asking questions about our criteria

for our entities, the way we ran with it like a diagnostic guide, like a ruler we could hold up against each other. I wonder how this plays into the losing game of authenticity. I'm curious what you think about it.

At the end of the day, we know we will be challenged. We prepare for it. There can be nothing they ask us that we haven't already asked ourselves. There can be no weak spot, no question that presses on a secret insecurity and buckles our knees. This is what fighting looks like, I think. This is how I get ready for the level of visibility I've chosen to hunt down so the work I make spreads like a contagious gospel. There can be no weapon they use against me that I haven't tried against myself first. It's a form of excavation, or interrogation at the very least. I knew people would ask why I was calling myself an ọgbanje, that they'd ask for proof, ask to be convinced. Which is really just them asking me to acknowledge power over me, that in order for my naming to be valid, they'd have to sign off on it. They don't. They don't even matter. None of this has ever been between us and them, it's between us and God and we know what we are, what we were made to be. When other Nigerians challenge me about calling myself Ala's child, I don't argue with them. I can't. That would be like saying their voices matter on this, and it's not possible. It's not a human issue; it's not a human's business.

You and I have talked about when you will uncover yourself to the humans to be the beast that you are—God in your mouth, an empire at your feet. You know you will be challenged. They will want to know on whose authority you speak, on whose authority you teach, who allowed you to do all this without an intermediary. You will have to remind yourself that it is on God's authority, and they will challenge that, too, because they are used to mediators, intercessors, and we are here saying we have direct lines, that we need neither permission nor guidance from humans. It must be galling for them, to prop up these men in their churches, these priests and pastors, only to have us ignore them. We have to be sure. We are sure when it's us, those who see each other, but it's harder when the humans bring their doubts and dismissals, heavy spells of their own whispering that we're crazy, we're making it up. I wrote to Eloghosa about how much work it took to tear off the years of believing their stories about us instead of our own. It's a constant practice, I think, to hold on to what we know is true even with human realities shrieking around us. It strengthens our centers, roots us deep in them, iroko trees planted by the waterside.

It is a different kind of power to be able to anoint yourself instead of kneeling for someone else to do it. We could spin out endlessly if we listened to their stories about how we aren't what we are—what would it be like to never forget that it was God who marked us directly and set us apart? The oil drips from our fingers onto our own foreheads. The world between us and God is the only real one. Maybe this is what madness is.

I can live with that.

Pain | Dear Daniel

don't like to write about this part, about the things that cracked my flesh, the hospital rooms and ambulances. I'm not even sure now that I've survived all of it. I thought it started after **Freshwater** came out, but Kathleen holds a memory of the summer before that, back when I stayed with her in Tanzania.

"You couldn't wash your hair because your neck hurt too much," she reminded me. I became a busy Venn diagram of hurts. One circle was the beating pulse of pain in the middle of my back, so loud that the simple brush

of fingertips over my skin made it scream.
Two doctors noted how unusual it was, that
localized acute whine. It sent ropes of ache
throughout the rest of my back; everything
was tired, everything hurt in different ways.
Hooks under my ribs, a spike living in my
tailbone, grinding its way up whenever I sat
down. Another circle was the aloneness, being
the wounded child no one would come for.
In the summer of 2018, I was on a plane back
from a birthday trip to Miami when swallowing became painful. I didn't pay much attention to it. The next morning, my neck and
shoulder hurt so badly that I couldn't sit up.
I had to roll onto the floor to get out of bed,
and then I found my way out of the apartment, took the A train to Fourteenth Street,
and started walking to Callen-Lorde.

Each step hurt, the right side of my body
was in agony, my arm dangling useless, my
body twisted. At the third-floor triage desk I
struggled to speak, my throat clamped shut
with pain. I was crying as I tried to lift my arm
to sign in and couldn't. The nurses called me
honey and got a doctor to see me immediately.
Everyone spoke gently. The doctor called an

ambulance to take me to the hospital; they put me in a wheelchair to bring me downstairs. I Facetimed my sister from the gurney. This was the day Bourdain died; I remember because the last time I'd been in an ambulance was after my suicide attempt in 2011, and being back in one while in so much pain made me think about dying all over again. Are suicide cascades a thing? I think they must be, somewhere. It's too much of a pull when one person does it.

That was one of the beginnings; I've been in chronic pain since that day. Even as I type this, my shoulder hurts. I did months of physical therapy. I'm still in acupuncture. Sometimes I worry that I'll never remember what a body without pain felt like. So much of it felt invisible and it had me looking for witnesses who could make it real in their eyes as well as mine. The weeks when I could barely leave my apartment, the depression from having a body that couldn't do the things it used to be able to, from gaining weight, from the pain that wouldn't go away.

This isn't going to be a long letter; I don't like writing it.

The constant hurt drove me further and further out of my own embodiment. Bassey became terrified that I wouldn't survive my bouts of suicidality—and I was scared too, which was new and especially bad. I'm never scared; I always think I'll survive, but this time I wasn't sure. There were so many reasons for it before, you know? I could say the depression was because I was broke, I didn't have a place to live, I couldn't afford therapy, but now I had a house. I had a fantastic therapist. My career was stable, with income programmed in for the next couple of years—and still I wasn't getting better. If anything, I was dying faster than before.

Bassey and I talked about medication. It wasn't an easy thing for me to consider; I'd fought against it for fifteen years. I wanted to be in control. I didn't want something else acting on my mind, bending it into new forms, bending me into new forms. I've been sober since 2012, not even by choice, just because my body started rejecting things one by one. Alcohol, dairy, meat, sugar, it all made me sick. I can't remember what triggered it—if it was the first surgery, or the autoimmune illness they couldn't diagnose, the one that attacked my joints and made it too painful to climb stairs. That one was intimate; I had never been so aware of the metatarsals in my feet before.

My favorite liquor used to be tequila, but I now avoid anything that alters my mental state. I can't smoke. I can't drink, same as you. My grasp on reality is already tenuous; it makes no sense to exacerbate it. I'm not allowed to alter myself that way. I can feel the instruction heavy on the back of my neck: I obey God's tongue. Besides, my flesh has already complied. Whenever I do try to take sips of alcohol, I can feel it in my blood; I can trace how it races through my vessels, my whole body roaring its arrival. When my last surgeon tried putting me on laughing gas for a minor procedure it felt the same way: contamination swirling through me as my mind watched it happen, apart and sober. Part of me is always sober. Even that one time I did shrooms, it was only amusing for a while to observe myself, and then I got upset when I couldn't make my body sober up to match the part of me that was watching. I didn't want medication to change me; I was already fighting so hard to hold on to myself. Bassey talked me down, and afterward, when the Prozac had rearranged things and taken the chokehold off my throat, I told her that she helped me save my life. It's the truth. Being medicated didn't feel like being drunk or high or on a trip. It felt like the opposite, like calm and clarity, like I could reach myself without chaos intervening and pushing me into death. It felt like **more** control, not less. A collar on the entropy of embodiment.

I am thinking about people who've helped me save my life. You sat with me in the emergency room at Ochsner Baptist more than once. The first time was when I dropped a knife on my toe and let it bleed nonstop overnight before I decided maybe someone should look at it. The second time was far more serious: three days into having a cyst rupture and bleed into my abdomen. I thought it was a stomach virus until they did the CT scan. That time, we were in the hospital for five hours. I've lost track of how many times I was sick in 2019: the bronchitis, the asthma, the suicidal bouts, the side effects of the antidepressants, the cyst, and of course the surgery.

For something that was such a pivotal

moment in my life, you'd think I'd want to write about it more. It's tedious and upsetting to look back on how hard it was to get the surgery, how I had to fire the therapist who wouldn't sign off on it by writing a letter for me. How even the next, "trans-friendly" surgeon made me jump through hoops to prove I was sane enough to get surgery when she'd crack cis people's jaws and noses apart with no question. How I grew more and more suicidal after confronting so many reminders that this world wants people like me dead. What else do you call it when you block access to life-saving health care, fucking bastards. It was a horrible stretch of time for me, a dark and cloying corridor, and I very much wanted to give up. It shouldn't have been this hard to get a double mastectomy. I pushed through—it was either that or suffer more—and found a new surgeon. I hate talking about surgeons, they are benevolent and yet terrible, but this one was good at what he did and, more important, he didn't believe in gatekeeping, so he didn't need a therapist's letter.

He did think it was weird that I wanted the nipples removed, but he didn't think it was dangerous or stupid—his words—so he agreed. We scheduled the surgery for June. Going under general anesthesia is interesting, because unlike dreaming, I don't go to another realm. I don't go anywhere. Everything just stops and starts back up, as if time was assassinated, as if I died. I imagine that this is what oblivion will feel like, an utter lack of awareness, a complete absence. Ann came down, and while I was in the operating room, she had a dream about walking into Shiny and seeing a small group of gorgeous people waiting for me to come back. It made me so happy, to know that the brothersisters had been waiting for me, and that they'd shown themselves to her. I'm always intrigued by how they present to people. I remember after we talked about me moving to New Orleans, you mentioned that they came to visit you, to check you out. You described them as large and aquatic. I imagined them in benevolent water spirit form, whales swimming through your house.

Recovering from the surgery took months. The knitting together of flesh was one thing, but the psychological effects of fundamentally reshaping my body were another. More than one person who did bodywork on me assumed I'd had breast cancer. I had nightmares about Nigerian gossip blogs finding out about the surgery before I'd decided to make it public. I was so tired. When they removed my drains, the plastic tubing snaked out from under my skin like worms. I wore a compression vest for weeks. I paid for the surgery in cash. I knew it was a righteous carving.

The day I decided that I needed to have another chest surgery, I had to do a radio interview for **Freshwater.** My host picked a passage for me to read out loud on air, and it was a section of the book I had forgotten about entirely.

We considered removing the breasts utterly and tattooing the flat of her chestbone, but that decisiveness still felt wrong, one end of the spectrum rocketing unsteadily to the other end— it wasn't us, not yet.

Not yet.

I didn't remember thinking, at the time, that I was ever going to have another surgery, but clearly it was known and recorded. There would be a time when the body would have to be carved to these specifications. Now that time had come and it was terrifying. I felt like I was advertising my deviance in a way that was so incredibly loud. I could never have a one-night stand again. Men didn't ask questions about the scars on my chest when I had small breasts, but this? This blankness, roped scars and no nipples? It would have to be a conversation, and I didn't want to talk to strangers about it. I could let them think I was a cancer survivor, but I don't live inside lies. I remember my ex-mother-in-law emailing me years ago when she saw pictures of me binding my chest with bandages, because she was upset that I did that with a "healthy" chest when she had survived breast cancer. More recently, when I wrote about reclaiming mutilation as an ọgbanje who had removed their uterus, an acquaintance objected to it by bringing up FGM in the comments. Cis women can be territorial about the strangest things.

A few weeks after my surgery, as you were killing a wasp in my kitchen, I told you how the procedure had been an unmasking, show-ing me as someone who had been hiding, exposing how much comfort I'd taken in a body that masked my deviance, and now I had gone and broken it all open. I was showing myself and it didn't feel safe.

"And," you added, "it's a mask you can't put back on."

And it's a mask I can't put back on. And that hurts. It feels raw and flayed and foreign. I am tired of this flesh, what it needs to feel right, what costs that comes with, the litany of ailments that march through its cells. I am tired of hurting, of spending months recovering from something or the other, bruised and swollen and exhausted. I want to be strong. I want to be free. I don't quite know what that looks like yet.

One night, while praying to Ala, I pause on a line in the prayer. Nara onyinye nkem. Accept my gifts, it pleads. I think of what I have given lately. I glimpse the surgery as another angle of obedience, turning into the slick, smooth snake chest, scars rubbing like scales.

I think I wanted to write this letter because the pain has been such an important part of these years. What story would be complete without it? People wait for me to get better, and

that doesn't really happen. I begin to understand the commitment of the word **chronic,**
the way it marries itself to you. I learn that I
will disappoint others with my lack of wellness, of capacity, of ability to explain to them
the intricacies of what the fuck is happening with my flesh that renders me unable to
perform the way I used to. I forgive myself
for letting people go, because I am trying to
hold on to myself. I learn to be okay with the
stories people have about me; some of them
might even be true. I don't need to be perfect
or liked all the time. The pain is demanding,
and it takes up a lot of space. I am a ragged
thing, and yet I have a community of people
around me who care for me when I am suffering, which is no small miracle. Maybe that's
something the pain has taught me—that I'm
not alone.

Someone sits with me in the ER for five
hours and we eat baos together afterward.
Someone drives me to the pharmacy as I bleed
through my shirt. Someone flies in from New
York, from Los Angeles, from San Francisco,
makes my eggs the way I like them, catches
my head when I collapse in the driveway so

my skull doesn't smash against the concrete. Someone oils my scalp and makes me butternut squash soup and stops me from driving to Target with drains in my chest because I wanted to buy a fake banana tree. Someone helps me wash my hair, builds shelving in my office, changes the pulls on my kitchen cabinets from steel to brass. I am a ragged imperfect entity, and yet there is a community that holds me when I am in pain. I didn't expect embodiment to come with grace like this.

I just wanted to say, thank you for being my friend.

Glory | Dear Tamara

always wanted to be famous.

When I first started writing for a living, it seemed like a decent avenue to accomplish this. I wanted to win all the prizes: a MacArthur, a Booker, a Pulitzer. The usual. Then, while I was briefly in the MFA program, there was this electric moment when it dawned on me that people who were famous were just . . . people. If they could reach that point, then so could I—and the possibility was terrifying. Lupita had just won an Oscar, I remember. I'd watched her in the series

MTV Shuga, and I knew people who'd gone to college with her. Something about being one or two degrees removed from an Oscar winner shook me, because it wasn't some far-fetched dream, happening to someone who only lived in a television screen. It was so close, I could breathe on it. I was twenty-seven, and there wasn't really anything stopping me from being thrown into the light I wanted. I was still a baby writer, but I knew that seeing the road as open meant I was admitting that this was possible for me. It wasn't floating in the sky, waiting to blind me as I gazed up from the ground. It was within reach—and all I had to do, incredibly, was write.

I started out in a community of young African writers, and we measured our potential by what the writers before us had achieved. If they had done it, then we could, too, and much of this was defined by awards. We could tell you every award Chimamanda had ever received; we calculated how long it took her to win a MacArthur, how old she was when she won the UK's Women's Prize. We dreamed of the Booker because of Ben Okri, the Nobel because of Wole Soyinka. We were ambitious and hungry; we wanted to be in those rooms, we wanted our names to be known on that level. In the months before **Freshwater** debuted, one of the first people who read the book—an author whose evaluation I valued deeply—told me she thought I was going to win a Booker. I was scared then, and the possibility made me feel a little safer, like I would be recognized and held in that.

Early on, however, a friend with decades of publishing experience had warned me that **Freshwater** wouldn't win any literary awards in the West. "They'll nominate you," they said, "because the book is too good to ignore. But they won't let you win, because you're not writing about Black abjection." When **Freshwater** was long-listed for the Women's Prize, the backlash that followed was transphobic and ugly. I knew it wouldn't make the short list; it's one thing for an awards committee to rock the boat with a long-list nomination for a Black trans author—that gets them points for inclusivity—but it's quite another to let it go as far as a win or even a short list. When the Booker nominations came out and **Freshwater** was absent, I was unsurprised. After the negative publicity the Women's Prize had received for my gender, I didn't think the Booker would want any of that smoke, not from the same book in the same year, not when there were safer choices with similar subject matter. "It's absolutely a gender thing," my friend agreed.

I thought about these costs, you know, when I disclosed that I wasn't a woman—even earlier, when I decided not to compare my work to the Western canon, when I made it clear that I was writing for people like me, not for a white gaze. There are always costs when you choose a center.

In coming to terms with embodiment as a god, I have accepted the desire for attention, for glory, for worship. It's been around since I was a child, and after years of trying to smother it with performed modesty, I've decided to leave it alone. It doesn't have to be a good thing or a bad thing; it can just be a thing. I had genuinely thought **Freshwater** would win a slew of awards. I don't think that's arrogant to say; I know what that book is. The first year of my career was a brutal one, because I realized that the shape of the success I'd predicted for myself was quite wrong, in interesting ways. It didn't look like awards, and that bothered me for months. I tried to remind myself that institutional validation was a complicated and problematic thing, that people were subjective no matter what, and that the structural bullshit that defines this country is not absent from these spaces. Part of me didn't care. I wanted to win. I wanted to stunt. I wanted the money and the prestige, the stage and the spotlight and the speeches. I'm a fucking god, I wanted the offerings. I wanted the power.

The magician talked me down. He reminded me that I wasn't in this to write the great American novel, but to make a body of work, so I would need a different standard of value. Other friends echoed the point, urged me to divest from award culture, dead those emotional bonds I was feeding with my want, my greed, my gleaming hunger. I knew they were right. When I cast questions to my spirits and deityparents, the answer has always been the same: to face my work. To make it, to protect it, fight for it, bring it to the people who need it. I keep myself whole so I can keep making the work—these books upon books that clatter inside my head, growling to be fed and written.

You've taught me so much about how aggressive we have to be with our wellness in order to survive the lives we're mapping out for ourselves. I want visibility so it can stretch as far as it needs to, and this kind of visibility is not free. It comes with costs: madness and paranoia and the partial death of privacy. It's ugly and difficult and I am an altar on a mountaintop, sacrificing myself to myself, to burn in a fire that the whole world can see.

The work is at once a service to the people I'm writing for, and a flex that will attract shine and power to me. Both can sit next to each other. I'm not ashamed to want the spotlight, because really, it's what makes me suitable for this job. What would be the point of telling stories like these and being amplified if it was just going to hurt you? It hurts me anyway, of course, but it's also what I wanted. Not entirely, not in a way that would consume my life, but enough to go through all this. The work is everything to me.

It's been difficult to disengage from award culture, though. It feels like having to reset and reset and reset again, over and over, dragging myself back to my appointed centers. At the same time, everything is easier at the center. All you have to do is write. The work is a beast on its own, a breathing thing that does its own work. It has a mouth and a voice. I saw this when I first signed with my agents, and then when I got the deal for **Freshwater.** I've never had to pitch this work, as in convince someone of it. All I've had to do is say what it was or let them read it. That's how we got the development deal with FX—you told them about the book, they read it, and they made an offer. We skipped the entire step of pitching it to people, and a new set of hungers yawned open in me. I want to win in every room I'm in. I have a tulle dress that's waiting for our series launch party. It has polka dots and is the most expensive item of clothing I ever bought. It is also a spell, sitting in a black garment bag in Shiny. We'll see how it works.

Recently, my therapist told me that I need to outline precisely what happiness looks like for me, so I'll recognize it when I get it. Before **Freshwater** came out, I thought award money would be my only chance at financial stability,

especially as a Black writer. We have to be excellent to even have a hope of surviving off
our work. A year after its debut, it hadn't won
an award, but I did have a book deal for half
a million dollars, and that was when I realized that I didn't just want the awards for the
money. I **had** the money, but I still wanted
the shine. I'm constantly resetting, remembering what's most important to me, remembering that sometimes success doesn't look
like what you've dreamed about—it looks
like goals that didn't even fit in your dreams.
I will take Shiny a thousand times over any
of the awards **Freshwater** was nominated for,
but let me remain honest about my desires. I
still want everything, except now I've learned
to shift it away from my center—to root it in
a periphery, where it belongs. Besides, I like
being alone too much to actually work toward
the shine; it's not a difficult formula to crack,
but it often involves entirely too much contact with white people and making things that
would be very boring for me. A god is still a
god, no matter what. My ontology isn't something fickle that depends on humans and their
loyalties, thank goodness. I am golden even

in isolation, perhaps especially then, my light bouncing off surfaces and amplifying itself off me.

I like writing this letter to you, because there is no shame in the magnitude of my wants when I'm talking to you. I never worry about sounding arrogant; I think I have accepted that I am, in fact, outrageously arrogant. So be it; what else would anyone expect from a god?

I look forward to us burning through the world together.

Undefeated | Dear Kanninchen

You were so afraid I would die.

My fears wear different faces. I'm afraid of suffering, of being trapped alive. Dying just hurts those left behind, it has nothing to do with me. I'll be gone, redundant. I imagine it will be what it was before I was born: nothing.

You once pointed out that death could be just more suffering, and in that moment I saw how vast the rift was between us: you creating a world where you suffer no matter where you turn, so why bother; me optimistic to the grave, believing in something better, even if

it's just oblivion. You told me how scared you
were of letting yourself into my apartment and
finding me covered in blood, in the bed, in the
tub. I was incapable of imagining your fear; I
haven't watched my loved ones stop breathing
the way you have. Still, you listened to all my
darkness and sat in it with me, holding my
hand. I never felt I was too morbid for you to
love—not until you told me that one of the
reasons you couldn't be with me was that you
were afraid of my relationship with death, of
the responsibility of keeping me alive.

I found that incredibly insulting. No one
asked you to keep me alive. No one asked you
to be a ventilator, a pair of hands desperate
against my sternum, a series of gasping breaths
into a slack mouth. You're not qualified. No
one is qualified. I am not a person who thinks
that anyone is coming to save me except myself. I have been dying my whole life, don't
you understand, flirting with death, bargain-
ing, stalling, shifting strategies to stay alive.
I am the person who is best at keeping myself alive, there is no singular love responsible
for me, there is no one who knows me deeper,
you would make a useless life jacket. You will

never be better at it than I am. All I wanted was someone for the loneliness, someone to hold my hand and sit in the dark with me.

All my worshippers flee at some point.

It has been like this for as long as I can remember—every once in a while, there comes a time when I have to step into a ring and fight Death. It's a recurring appointment, with no pattern and no proxies. You can't fight it for me, you can only watch from outside the ropes and I know that is a terrifying place to stand, helpless and with futile hands. I know that, every time, it looks like I'm going to lose. I stay in bed for five days, watching **She-Ra and the Princesses of Power** while my soul spars. I chant over and over, words I don't remember, garbled prayers. Death is friendly, casual with its grin. It is patient, it knows that no matter how many fights we have, it will win the last one. Each time, I fight for my life. Each time, it fights for sport, out of habit, for destiny.

I have been alive for more than thirty years; I am undefeated in this ring. I wish you could see that about me—not when I am struck down and bleeding against the floor, begging it to take me, to end the pain and free me from the flesh. I wish you could see the tenacity I have, the iron jaw locked onto life, the fact that Death has never won, that I am a champion in one of the most brutal games anyone could be playing.

I thought you were on my team, my family, my ace. One of the people who worked with me to make sure I spent as much time out of the ring as possible. We talked in a restaurant in Jackson Heights about how your father fought Death, too, what it was like for you and your mother to love people who had these battle appointments with a reaper, how your father trained you to fight when you were young, making you so well prepared that Death didn't bother to keep a standing appointment with you. You were trained by an expert. I learned on my own. I learned how to stay alive when the assassin lives in my own head, how to fight an opponent who has already seduced me before the round starts, an opponent who can read my mind. Everyone else has always been more scared than I am, and it confuses me sometimes; don't we all lose in the end, anyway? I am an old fighter and a very young child.

I thought you were on my team.

In the end, it takes days of cornering you for you to tell me the truth, that you slept with her, got her pregnant, moved her into your house, and lied to me about it for months. There are likely many more secrets you kept, a thousand more lies. As this truth leaves your mouth, I feel you lift my body—the body you've held against yours so many times, telling me how small it was, how fragile, the body you've worshipped and bathed and oiled—I feel you lift it and toss it into the ring like a rag doll. Death looks up, surprised, an unexpected fight suddenly bloodied into its calendar. I am scrambling up, terrified and disbelieving, my hands bruised with wailing hurts: the promises you'd broken, the deceit you'd maintained, the betrayal of your eyes through the ropes of the ring. I make excuses for you; I call myself collateral damage, because I believe you when you say you didn't think about what the deceit would do to me, that you were wrapped up in your own terror. I have a nasty habit of believing you even though you keep lying to me, because there is a sweet kid in me who cannot understand how you could love me and lie at

the same time. "It's not always about you," you
say, while Death lopes toward me with that
casual grin, and I don't know which is worse:
that I'm back in the ring or that you're the one
who threw me in, or that you're pretending
you're not a liar and a traitor. I almost go mad.
I go mad a week later.

Here is the thing, my love, my magician.
There is something I know about you: a truth
you let slip once in a while, a truth you bury
deep in an iron cage in your belly because it
would be so inconvenient if people remembered it. You are completely self-aware. You do
not forget things. If at any time you say you
don't remember, you are lying. If you say
you don't know what people want or you
didn't think about something, you are lying.
You think about everything all the time. You
know everything about yourself. You are deeply
ashamed of it, and for good reason, but instead
of trying to be better, you hide and lie. But
I remember you, and I remember every time
you accidentally told me the truth about who
you are, that you think through every consequence of everything you do before, during,

and after you do it. **You know.** The biggest lie you ever tell is that you don't know.

I see you, my love. I always paid attention to you. And you see me. You know me inside out—you know every single thing that could hurt me, you knew how the fear that hunted me the most was of someone I love lying to me, maintaining the lie over time, touching and smiling at me during the whole thing, mocking my world. I know how easy it is for people to do. I've fucked a married man in a threesome in my apartment on his birthday while his wife texted him sweet thoughts, thinking he was at the doctor's. I fucked him in their bed. I was the one who saw their baby take his first step, after the wife had banned me from their home. We played house in a whole different country, and everyone said how the baby looked just like me. I married a man who cheated on his girlfriend with me for years, I stopped bothering to remember the rest. **I know how easy it is.**

I didn't think anyone would love me without doing that to me and that's why I chose to be the secret, the affair, the one who was in on the joke—because my terror was that, if I didn't, I would be the person being lied to. Where were the loves that weren't laced with lies? Everyone made it seem so normal; I didn't think I had a choice, other than to pick what side of the con I'd be on. You kissed me in the park, and when I laughed with delight, you told me you always wanted to hear me make that sound, and you lied from the start, especially about her, that you were with her, that she'd been living with you for years, you called yourself a house built of lies and you promised to change. You said it would be a privilege to spend the rest of your life making it up to me. I thought I was being tested. I have always been a gullible child. I wanted to love you hard enough to pass the test.

But then you went and threw me in the ring instead, and honestly, I understand why it took you so long to tell the truth—with people like me, there is only one moment to be honest, one window to come clean. As soon as you miss it, everything only becomes more and more of too late. The lie inhales and starts to grow. When is a good time to destroy your best friend? You missed the window, I think out of anger—not because I left, but because I had the nerve to come back. You'd already fucked her. You knew I might be hurt, but I wouldn't think you'd done anything wrong. We both remember London. We make choices in these windows: to fight, to be brave, to look truth in the face, to hope that we can still come back from this. In my return, you chose—whether you admit it or not—the one thing you absolutely knew would hurt me back, wound me as deep as your pain goes. You lied, my magician. I trusted you arm-deep in my chest, and you used that to harm me further than anyone ever has. No one else ever loved or knew me enough to be this kind of threat.

So. I am in the ring, Death bearing down on me, and there you are, crying in my apartment for yourself. Not for me, for yourself. I find it interesting. I comfort you because there is a hurting little boy in you I wish I could have saved. I wonder if you realize that withholding the truth took away my choices. I never knew enough to give informed consent. When I go mad, I ask you if you feel like a rapist yet, because I want you to think of how I would have made different choices with my body if you had told me the truth. There's no need to look at me like that, all aggrieved. You were the one who called me soft; I have always called some of me cruel.

I am in the ring. You are making silly arguments, claiming you'd set clear boundaries about us never being together. You are lying. You said we should have been married by now. I see you holding me in the back of the taxi while I sobbed.

"You tried with all these others, why couldn't you try with me?" I asked.

"What do you think trying looks like?" you said, frustrated but gentle. "It looks like this."

I sniffled and looked up. "Like, you're just not ready yet?"

"Yes," you said, "yes, I'm just not ready."

I wanted to be good at loving; I wanted to pass the test. You held me in the curve of your body in all three of my beds, ran your hands over my thighs, ground your hips, and told me I was your entire sexuality now. The whole time, she was a mile and a half away in the house you never let me enter, pregnant with your child. You are worse than a cruel person, you are a coward. If you are going to be brutal, do not pretend to be soft. It is the least you can do. Or, when you drop the mask of softness, hold your brutal chin up, look at me with your brutal eyes. I have done terrible things, and I knew they were terrible. I loved that they were terrible, and I showed it openly. You are such a fucking coward.

I am in the ring. Death slides a hand around my neck, and you are crying for yourself. I am Lot and his family, you are an entire city on fire, I cannot look back; my arm is turning to salt just from writing this. When I go mad, I tell you I can make your nightmares come true, too. I tell you to wait and see. I keep my promises.

I am curious. Do you think throwing me in the ring was less an attempt on my life than if you had held me down with one hand and beat me senseless with the other, till my cheekbones cracked, till my eyes swelled shut, till my lips split and teeth fell out, blood over your skinned knuckles, over and over, until I was limp in your grasp like the corpse you've imagined me to be? You let the ring do the dirty work for you, but I don't think it's very different, my love. How will you punish me for this letter, for the sin of making you look at yourself?

My friends couldn't leave me alone for the first twenty-four hours. They took shifts to keep me alive, to make sure I survived the ring, the surprise round belled open by a traitor. They came every day to watch over me. You knew it would be this bad, and you did it anyway. I don't need to make a litany of all the ways you fucked me over, because I know your secret: you already know all of it. Do you feel the shame? I'd rather you felt pleasure— a filthy pleasure in being seen for what you are. I'd rather you licked my tears off my face and whispered that you meant every moment of hurt you caused. I'd rather you boast about how you flayed me perfectly, blindfolded, with one arm tied behind your back, while focusing on something else, an effortless skinning. You always liked me raw under your hands.

The only point to this letter is the looking. My former beloved, my hurt monster, you can blind everyone else, trick us with glamours and masks, but you're not capable of ripping out your own eyes, may your mirrors haunt you. I just wanted to tell you that I see you, and I cannot be around you because you basically tried to kill me, and that I love you so very much. I want to tell you I forgive you, and never come back to my light until you are clean enough to be seen. You turned your face away from your god. I do not envy the darkness you have thrown yourself into; I do not know what shreds you will be left in. I am not worried about myself. Even like this, betrayed and skinned, crawling in bloodsplatter, my shrines broken, my trust swinging bloated and black from your neck, I am still me. I am still a god. I remain, as always, undefeated.

Grief | Dear Eugene

Your play brother is a liar.

I know I said he wouldn't lie to you, but don't listen to me. I'm a soft gut people love to rip open, as if there's something about that underbelly skin they have radar for—the way it doesn't armor up against them, perhaps, the way they can sink deliciously deep, the gasping dark of the blood that runs out, the metal of it thick and victorious in their noses. I don't know; you'd have to ask him. He lied to me for months, a deceit that grew exponential and swollen. This is not a letter about that. This is a letter about me—all these letters are about me—but this is a particular me, standing with loops of my own viscera staggering and sliding over my shocked hands, watching him cry as he leaves my apartment, his right arm slick with my blood, up to his elbow.

It hurts so much, Eugene. The grief attacks me indiscriminately. It scrambles through my bamboo blinds in the mornings—the ones he put up—and presses me into my pillows, weighing me down with morning light and the confusion of waking up into a world where, for one heartbreaking moment, I've forgotten what happened. Remembering is the death of mercy. Sometimes it comes at night, when I realize how gone he is, when his ghost kneels blindfolded at the edge of my bed. I send ragged voicenotes into my phone and my friends try to hold me as best they can from the distance that splits us apart. I try not to cry too loudly, in case the neighbors hear, but this is Brooklyn. They probably don't care. I wonder what my apartment's sound track is like from the outside: gospel music, hoarse sobbing, **The Great British Baking Show,** the soft roar of the air conditioner, silence, an injured god keening **have mercy, have mercy** while the stovetop hisses soft blue fire under a copper pan. I take my anxiety meds to stave off the panic attacks, and to my relief, they work. I change my life because it is different without him in it. He was my family, he is dead, he is literally down the street with her and their baby, he is a ghost painting green leaves on a blush wall in my bedroom. I dissolve our ties. I give my landlord notice that I am leaving this apartment; I don't tell him it's haunted. The ghost only targets me, after all; future tenants will be safe. I throw out the material evidence of how I loved him: his toothbrush and toothpaste (he doesn't like my Sensodyne), the Reese's cups in my fridge (when he's sad, he eats junk food), the LED lamp by my daybed (my ceiling light was too dim for his work). I rip up notes and ticket stubs and sketches on random notebook paper. I don't burn them or drown them or do anything particularly meaningful with them. I just throw it all in the trash and put it out on the street. I am just cleaning.

There are a slew of emotions that come tangled up in grief, that invade when a person you love dies that halfway death—the kind where they're still walking around with an audacity of a body, while simultaneously existing as a ghost that shows up in corners of your house and makes you cry. One of them is sadness, another is loss, another is relief. I was glad to be free of him, this love that would not take me but would not let me go. Another was hope: the edges of another life that could be clear and honest and, perhaps most of all, brave. The night he was at my place confessing his lies, after I screamed and wept and fought the urge to throw glass, he asked me what he could do to make amends for the harm he'd inflicted on me. I asked him for three things: the first was to get help and the second was to send me the art he owed me. That made me think of you and me outside the hotel, teasing him about what he owes us, the way you smelled when I hugged you goodbye, the sudden sharpness with which I always want you, since that first dinner in the booth, these fine blades of desire piercing me in a thousand places.

Then I smiled at him, his hands in mine, and I asked for the third thing. "Eugene," I joked. He nodded, teary-eyed, as if it would save him. "I will," he said. He knew that's not what I was asking; you are no one's to give except yours. I just wanted your play brother to give his blessings if you ever had reason to need them, whether you asked or not. I know how ridiculously presumptuous this sounds, but I always worried that you'd assassinate a chance of anything between us out of loyalty to him. You have to understand, he and I had talked about it quite a bit, what you and I would be like together; he'd just mentioned that you might be ending things with the dreamskin woman. Ignore me, I'm spinning worlds again, a silver story out of faint threads. This is still a dream where you want me back. I'm writing this letter because I want you to know the truth about why I left him and what he did to me, and I'd rather tell you now than relive it later. You don't have to do anything. None of us do.

When I asked him for that, I was afraid. Standing there with my intestines slipping down my legs and a joke in my mouth, I was afraid that he would not only break my heart but also take the sliver of this dream into the back and blow its brains out. I hoped, instead,

that he might tell you what he once told me—
how he thought you and I might fit well together, how he saw potential for care there,
how he thinks I'd challenge you. I have no
idea what he's capable of anymore. Neither
do you, trust me—lovers see a different set
of knuckles than the ones you dap. Or don't
trust me. I'm no prophet, just a believer with a
regenerating underbelly.

I wondered if you knew the whole time, if
you were in on it, smiling to my face at the last
dinner while I sat next to him, still holding a
love I didn't know had turned on me. What
else could you do but be loyal and hold his
secrets? Does it mean a bullet to this dream?
Maybe this dream needs to be put down anyway. We don't talk about how stories can be
used as drugs enough, highs to disappear into.
That doesn't mean it's not real.

I tell him I forgive him. I write him a letter
and all it does is look him straight in the face,
even though I know how much he hates it
when I do that. It feels strange to read my last
letter to you. I can see so much hesitation in
it, such a fear of hurting him with this desire.
For the first few days, my grief cuts through

desire's throat, leaving it exsanguinated. It becomes hard for me to imagine wanting someone who still loves him after what he did to
me—which is ironic, because I still love him,
even after what he did to me. I guess what I'm
saying is that I can't imagine you holding him
accountable for the harm he caused. I believe
you look up to him, and I wonder how many
of his failings you see. Maybe more than I did.
I've heard how you talk about your boys; the
devotion is thick and heavy there. I remember
sitting in the car listening to the stories about
helping each other unlearn toxic behavior, but
I wonder what your protocol is for when your
boys harm others. I wonder if you've harmed
women, or entities like me, and how you handle accountability. I'm sorry, I don't mean to
sound judgmental. I genuinely don't know
y'all like that, and it's not my business. I would
protect my family too, I just . . . I thought he
would protect me.

I think I'm writing this letter because I want
someone from his world to be a witness to
what happened, to what it did to me.

You don't know me either. All I do is shape

a hologram of you out of words, project you into these letters. You've barely met me; you've loved him for almost half your life. But don't mind me, you are an entire person beyond what even he sees of you, beyond a few conversations I overheard. I'm just a gutted god—a small Prometheus under siege from shape-shifting eagles. I swear, I did not expect your play brother to turn into one of them.

I'm forgiving him because I don't have time to hold a grudge, because I see how fear and cowardice have a chokehold on him, because there is no penance he could perform that would bring him more suffering than what he's doing to himself. I say this with all the tenderness I ever held him with. I forgive him because I believe in his rehabilitation, should he ever choose it, although I don't think he will. I don't think he will, and it feels so absolute, so ruined and final. But I found the space to write you this letter in forgiving him. I still want him to be loved, I wonder if it helps to have people who see him the way I used to, as someone better than he is. I wonder if he can live up to it instead of wearing it as a mask. I wonder what you will do, but you don't have to do anything, and you certainly don't have to tell me any of it.

I did everything I could.

Through my grief, I inhale this as fact, like it can hold my lungs together. I loved him past common sense. I loved him like a god does, as if I could not die, with worlds living and expiring in my mouth. I don't have time for mourning, but my God, how mourning makes time for me. In an older story, I would have thought I could've done something better, something different. I would have painted myself as unlovable, as if that would explain why these devastations migrate so brutally into my chest. He's at least the third man I've loved who's tried to teach me how much I was worth with one hand, while hurting me with the other. I learn fast, though. I wonder if they think I won't apply these lessons to them, if they're surprised when I do.

Your play brother was a good teacher. He helped me see myself—he would tell me how soft I am, how tender and open, he would say it with wonder in his voice, looking at me like I was a sun he would willingly let blind him.

But then he went ahead and eviscerated me anyway, and it was so **easy.** It was so easy, Eugene, for precisely those reasons, my ready pulp. You cannot begin to imagine how many times I've been broken open, spilled on someone's floor, left with their greedy handprints seared all over my exposed and panicking heart. But look, this time, I'm not bothering to knit things back together. I don't want to change. There will be no hastily manufactured armor, no walls thrown up around my heart. This letter is a piece of that. I am exhausted. I am a split fruit, leaking sweetness. I am a fucking god. I still want you, delicate gold on your chest, thick ink on your knuckles, I still want to drip down your hands. I still want you in my mouth, velvet and salt. Perhaps that, too, is part of the grief. It's not a bad way to look for life when surrounded by half-deaths and ghosts.

This sorrow spills large like dark rainbow oil: that we live in a world where being loved is more terrifying than not, where your play brother could do this to me—**to me**—because it hurt him too much to be seen. I wish the world had been gentler with all of us.

I wrote this because I thought you might understand something of how this is such a dying for me. I just wanted to be his friend, Eugene, but he broke things so completely that there's no way I can put them back together. Anyone who can make worlds that well can destroy them just as easily. I miss him like I lost one of my senses. It will pass, with time, but I wanted to tell you. I wanted you to know the truth, even if just for the sake of a dream. I wanted to give you more than he gave me. You are beautiful enough for that.

Thank you for listening.

Resurrection | Dear Yshwa

I died from rage.

I won't lie, it started because I wanted to punish the magician. I wanted his nightmares to do what they do best, trigger the bogeyman of fear that keeps him trapped in his head, set off that churning of guilt and shame—yes, you're so broken that you ruin everyone else's life. Yes, you drove the person you love to this mad dance in a hotel room, pouring a cocktail into a low, wide glass when they've been sober for seven years, playing Amadou and Mariam from a phone propped in another glass so the sound reverberates, tinny and shrill, "Sabali" on an eternal loop, greasing open the gates of death so we can finally walk through. I wanted to hurt him, but he's not who I was angry at, not really. Yes, there was pain and there was grief, but rage was the thing forcing the gates open. How many times? How many times were the gods, all of you, my deityparents and siblings, how many times were you all going to make me suffer in this useless fucking flesh and then forbid me to leave it? How dare you. How dare you keep me from home. How dare you assume that I would always be compliant, obedient, that I would stay like a fucking dog because you told me to. I am a god, too, you know, I am madness itself.

I'd spent so much of my life being good, the good child, the good incarnation, doing what I was supposed to do, which was obey and live. I wanted to be soft; I thought you all would spare me if I became soft and tender the way you made me. Instead I was left gutted, bleeding, turned into an altar, because it's never enough for you, is it?

It's such a human thing to think this was

between me and the magician. It never is. I
don't waste my grudges on flesh.

So. I decided to be defiant, and I used my
rage at the magician to unlock a deeper fury, a
fury I didn't think I was allowed to feel, a spit
in the face of God fury, a rebellious well you
think you can keep me here against my will,
I will make—for the first time ever—a good-
faith attempt to destroy the vessel you tossed
me into type of fury. I knew there could be no
wavering. This would be no bluff; you cannot
bluff against God. If I decided to do this, I
knew the kind of magic I would have to weave
to execute it. Death is a difficult spell when
you turn it inward.

First, everything has to become unreal. You
have to kill the world around you so it doesn't
interfere. You can't afford to think about how
your little sister will feel when she finds out
she's alone now, how your human mother will
crack when she knows she failed to keep you
alive, how it's not just the magician's fears you
will be bringing to life by dying. These are
distracting thoughts; they will sabotage the
work you're trying to do. So everyone has to

disappear, there is nothing except the room and the music and the rest of reality bleeds into emptiness.

This is strong magic, to destroy an entire world so you can be free enough to destroy a body.

I do it sober. The cocktail I drink is merely to welcome the pills rattling in a glass, orange and green and teal and white, like a bowl of candy waiting to stop a heart. I can induce a trance without anything; I don't need substances. This is just worldbending pulled into tight focus, it only needs concentration to hold everything steady as I drink mouthfuls of pills with a bottle of orange juice. I stand on the couch and press my hands to the glass of the hotel window. The Hollywood sign shows up against the hills. I dance through the room; I have had a good life. I am going home. The song loops and loops, the words are in French and Wolof. I know it is a message from the brothersisters, I can feel when they're sending songs—calling me stubborn, telling me to be strong. I wonder what this one is. I look up the translated lyrics; they are singing about patience, how the world is for amusement, how we came to have fun. They are sending me kisses and calling me baby and I know I should bend. I know I should listen to my siblings warning me that I am here for life, that we are here for life, but I'm just mad that they're trying to stop me. I don't even care that they're doing it gently. If I was sad, maybe it would have worked, but I am enraged, and I have decided and I am stubborn, so I will finish this thing I have started. I start dancing again.

I dance until all the pills are gone. I wish I could say I thought of you, Yshwa, but I didn't. You weren't part of that world I was making. I thought of my papa, the Baron, as if I could force his hand with this grave. I am not despairing. I am not hopeless. I am furious and if you all love this body so much, fuck you. Fuck you for putting me in it. Fuck you for asking me to endure this much torture. Who told you a human life was worth this, it is nonsense, rubbish, I am trying to throw it away. None of you should have brought me here. I change into my favorite pajamas: pink trousers and a wraparound tunic top, green foliage drifting across them. I want to look good when they find me. When Ann finds me. The world wavers at that thought, but I reinforce it. Ann is not human. She will know why I had to leave. I hope someone else finds the body, a stranger. It doesn't matter who finds it, I won't be here anymore. I let go of all time that stretches beyond this and now. I get into bed and start reading a book, waiting for un-consciousness to come and collect me.

I make it through a chapter before I can feel the heaviness stalking through my limbs, the grams of medication I took doing their work in my bloodstream, in my brain, in my gut and heart. I have always wanted to go to sleep and never wake up. Now, it's here and I am ready. I turn off the light and snuggle into the hotel bed, my eyes closing, oblivion wrapping kind arms around me. Everything dissolves and I am gone. That is how I died.

Three hours later, I woke up.

Now, I want to ask how it was for you on the third day, Yshwa. How did your body feel? I had to pee; it was my body that woke me up. I stumbled to the bathroom, and afterward I lay down again and thought things through. Has anyone ever asked you what happened in the cave before they rolled back the stone?

Did you take a moment to yourself, to run an account of how your body was beating when it shouldn't have been? Did you talk to God? I didn't. I knew I had failed; I knew that a reckoning was coming and that it was coming quickly. I called Ann and told her what happened, then called Alex. I got dressed to go to the emergency room. My speech was slurred. It had been long enough for the drugs to soak into my system; what was done could not be undone. I packed my phone chargers and told Tamara what had happened. Later, she said I was so calm that it took her a long time to realize I was in the middle of the crisis, not the aftermath. The Uber took a long time to come. I swayed in front of the hotel like the top of a palm tree. I made small talk with the Uber driver—hilarious, I thought, for someone who was either dying or coming back to life. I couldn't stand in the emergency room. They made me fill out forms.

Ann met me there and it was my first time seeing her new haircut. It's gorgeous on her. The nurse called me in and helped me into a wheelchair when I started collapsing.

We stayed in the hospital for twenty hours.

Ann helped me in the bathroom. My arms started convulsing and didn't stop for four weeks. I could control it if I focused, like most things in this reality. I threw up a few times. I became short of breath and they tried to put an albuterol mask on me, but it made me throw up again and hyperventilate. So many people came in and out. Time bent. There were IVs and blood and potassium tablets. It was too late to pump my stomach. They tried to transfer me to inpatient care, but Ann and I bent the world until eight hours later, the on-call psychiatrist came in and discharged me. He was a lovely German man. No one thought he would let me go. That is a different letter—about humans and institutions and violences from people who love me, because they are afraid of things I am not afraid of. My life doesn't belong to any of them.

I complained to Ann about how we could've been shopping, going to Little India or the pottery place, and she pointed out that God was grounding me. The message was clear, Yshwa, I received it well. I am not allowed to die. I can try as much as I want, but it will always end like this, having to fight humans for my freedom, my body thrown into their hands, and that is a terrible punishment in and of itself. Everyone was there telling a story of me being broken and fragile. They don't understand the rage that came with it. They don't understand that it's just a fucking life. Before this, I would have said that it was mine to do with as I wished, but I learn lessons well. It's not mine; I just have custody for now, for this lifetime. It's God's, and if God says I can't throw it away, then I can't throw it away. I felt relieved afterward. I apologized to the loved ones who were hurt, but if I could go back, Yshwa, I would absolutely die all over again. Would you?

I needed to be that angry. I needed to try. You cannot be truly submissive with a low and furious resentment rotting deep in your heart, buried by performances of obedience and the meek quiet of a good subject. Even you: you shouted when you were on the cross, you shouted against God. I needed to scream beyond voice, to defy heaven and the deity-parents, to flail and tear the vessel apart from the inside out. Heaving in the aftermath, I could hear God's voice, patient and wry: "Are you done now?"

You can call it a tantrum if you want.

I did get it out of my system, violently and under medical supervision. The day after, I was high and manic, clarity blazing through me like an angel's sword. I tried to explain how it felt to lie down and meet darkness, expecting to die, the surrender of that. I've never given myself over so completely. I've always fought it—called for help, told someone, followed the rules to stay alive. This time, I was giving up a life, sacrificing everything that everyone said I had or would have. I put myself on the altar and used myself as the knife, there was no intercession of a ram, the offering was not stopped. And yes, it was done out of rage and spite, but to return a life to God is to return a life to God: it takes effort, it takes commitment. It's hardly surprising that an offering made with that kind of intent would be thrown right back in my face, but my point is that I lay down to die and I woke up.

You know, Yshwa, but I don't think many of

the humans understood how freeing that was. I'd lived so much of my life with the reaper's blade hovering over my neck, longing for death and fearing it in equal measure. I flirted with pills and overdoses, afraid they would work, afraid they wouldn't. That evening, I faced the largest threat to my life and I tried to lose. I threw myself against the blade, faced Death in the ring and didn't fight. I embraced it and pressed my soul against its robes. Take me, I commanded, cut away the flesh. I did all that and I lived.

I lived.

Was I ever really in danger in the ring? I was suffering, to be sure. I begged Death enough times to make it end. But this time it wasn't me surrendering with a bent neck, moving my hair away from my spine in defeat; this time Death had to throw me off and I realize that it has never been allowed to reap me. How can you die if the Baron won't dig your grave, if Ala won't swallow you down, if God commands that you live? So. I lived and I will live. How reckless I intend to be, how unafraid. I slept with death creeping in my veins and I woke up. Nothing can stop me if death cannot.

They should all be afraid of what I can do now, Yshwa, I have nothing left to fear.

On the second morning, I packed up to leave for the airport. I had never seen my face so pale. I wondered if it was the hotel mirror, the brilliance of the inset light, but no, there was chalk under my skin and darkness bruised beneath my eyes. Did you look like this when you resurrected, Yshwa? Or were you bright before you disappeared? Your body only needed to be animated briefly, and then you left. I wonder if it would have been different if you'd still had a lifetime left, if you needed to keep the body for that long.

A week later, I stepped out of my car and collapsed in the driveway of the godhouse. My arm convulsed for weeks—the body glitching from its proximity to death. I am regenerating, healing the vessel from the violence it experienced, from the violence of existing, the first and myriad violences that tremble through it.

I am ready to be obedient. I have no resentment against God left; there is such peace in surrendering to a will that is so much greater than yours, relief in rebelling so fiercely and being quashed so thoroughly. I am a good soldier, despite my brattiness. Did you feel like a soldier? You were sent, you had a mission, you were even disguised in flesh. You followed your orders to the death and beyond.

How do you live after you die? Like a haunting or like a second life? If you were a thing that was born to die, then you were a dead thing even in your first life. Can the people around you tell that you are even more dead now than you were before? Can they see the ways you've changed, how being taken this far away from them contaminates you with distance even after you return? I was so unseen before; I cannot imagine how much more unseen I will be now, in what directions my heart will break again. It doesn't matter. I am a good soldier.

I am ready to be obedient.

Marks | Dear Jahra

I think I might give myself stigmata like Yshwa's—scars from a short death, the five holy wounds. Black circles on my hands and feet, a gash of ink on my side. I am holy, a saint, a reborn god. After I died and came back, I tattooed the flat of my chest as I had predicted in **Freshwater.** I wrote DEAD THING under the solid triangle on my sternum (the only constant is change) and took marks from the Baron's vèvè, inking them into the skin above my pectoral muscles. The new tattoos formed an inverted triangle, with the solid original sitting upside down at the apex. I put one of my godnames on my wrist: EKWUEME, the one who says and then does. The one who keeps their word, really, the one who turns intentions into prophecies because the words come true. We've talked about tattooing as a way of reminding ourselves of what we are. Does embodiment come stained with forget-fulness? If we mark the vessel enough, will it remember what it is?

I know now that I'm required to surrender— to life, to this flesh and all it comes with, to these brief decades of existence—but it's still a difficult thing to hold on to. It slips through my fingers like water, mercury, blood. I tat-too the word OBEDIENT on my knuckles, to remind myself of what I am. I don't post it on social media because I'm not sure I want to talk about being so deeply religious, not yet. Everyone would assume I'm Christian and I'm not, despite my relationship with Yshwa. I try to pray every night, first to God, the big one, the one that covers the rest with a shadow. Then to my chi, asking it for good things, to remove every evil thing in my heart, to bring me wealth. Then to my deitymother,

Ala. Sometimes I talk to the brothersisters and to the Baron. I wrap my arms around Yshwa's neck and look for home in his skin. What it is like to be a god who worships other gods?

My altar is thrown together and symmetrical. A bottle of palm wine. A white candle on a brass candlestick molded in the shape of a coiled and rearing snake. A tray full of salt and petals and crystals that Katherine put together for me. A ceramic bowl with congealed palm oil. A closed jar of habanero peppers soaking in rum. Some dried rosemary. I wish I could grow yam in my garden, boil it, and offer it to Ala like I used to when I lived in Trinidad. I had a shrine for her outside then, at the base of a large tree where I would sit out in the mornings. I haven't found the right place for the shrine here yet. I started growing a grove of banana trees in the back, but they've gone brown from the frost.

When I was in Trinidad in 2016, I did a ritual to mark myself. I cut vertical lines into my face and packed them with ash. Back in the day, my people used to mark ọgbanje children after they died. There were multiple purposes for this: to identify the child when it came back, but also to alienate it from its brother-sisters. Their theory was that once the cohort saw that the ọgbanje could no longer be stealth, could no longer pass for human because its face had been marked, then the cohort would reject the ọgbanje and it would resort to becoming human. What is an ọgbanje without its cohort, after all? Who wants to be alone like that?

But imagine how different things are now, because now is not then. Imagine a cohort that is loyal; imagine a world where an ọgbanje doesn't have to hide, where it marks itself because fuck a human and a mutilated corpse. What is it like to be so fearless as to advertise openly? The scars on my face were an exercise, but they never raised. I was surprised—scars on my chest always hypertrophy—but I suppose these were too shallow. Instead I tattooed them in, black lines on each cheekbone. I am interested in the way we put permanent reminders into the skin, into the flesh. Does it actually work? I find that my marks seep into me, that I forget what it was like to have a body before the marks, it is as if they have always been there. I adjust so easily.

My first set of knuckle tattoos were split—
the word MMỤỌ on my right hand, a collection of Nsibidi symbols on my left. The mark
for python. The mark for the source of the
spring. The marks for water, star, bridge, and
knife. A bridge between worlds: all freshwater comes out of the mouth of a python;
we are knives cutting through the world; and
Asughara is a double-edged dagger. An alter-
nate translation for the symbol for star was ce-
lebrity, which I liked as a prophecy. I got this
set in Vietnam and they sank into my skin and
I forgot that they were reminders. Writing this
helps me remember.

Maybe I should be meditating on myself,
on each thing I've drawn into this container
of flesh. I am curious about your marks and
how they relate to your embodiment, how
they serve as reminders, how they hold you
while you breathe. I wonder if there is ever
going to be enough I could do to my skin that
would render me recognizable when I look
into a mirror.

After my surgery, the new scars marked
my chest in raised and jagged lines. The surgeon is injecting them with steroids to flatten

them out. Their topography doesn't bother me; I'm just curious to see what they'd look like flat, and the steroid shots are free. The main scars are orbited by smaller scars, scattered constellations. I'm not sure what caused those—stitches, perhaps, as they migrated and dissolved within my chest. I have marks in the crook of both my elbows, scars that really shouldn't be there, so of course that makes me only more interested in why they showed up. They're from the IVs in the emergency room after my resurrection in LA, small brown smudges darker than the surrounding skin.

All these marks add up to a map of sorts: different phases of embodiment like a shifting moon, different places, different hurts. I am looking forward to my final death, and what the body will look like then, how the map will have changed. I imagine it expanded, thickened, lost in folds. I think I will have them burn it then, turn all my marks into ash. They were mine; they should be gone when I am. This body was a home that took me decades to surrender to, and now I am decorating it with a different kind of intention, as if it's a weapon, because it holds my spirit.

Our conversations are a gift, to be able to speak as I think, without translation, knowing that I am seen and heard and understood. I hope this letter reaches you well. Give my love to Connor.

Guard | Dear Katherine

Consider me a bruise, a swollen wound, purpled and puffy.

I wish that would inform how people brush up against me in this world, how they touch me, the pressure with which they press. Marguerite tells me often how strong I am, and how fragile. I'm not interested in resilience, but in how to move through this world with reciprocal tenderness, even though this only works with people interested in the same thing. It's fine. I've never been the type of god to waste time on attempted conversions.

We've talked briefly about the paranoia that develops in times like this, and I wonder if it counts as paranoia when it's warranted—the shields we have to throw up, the calculations of harm we have to make, predicting where we will need to be protected. My therapist wants me to trust my own assessments instead of consulting my friends, because I tend to believe them more than myself. I've spent most of my life watching the world try to convince me that it's not doing anything to me, that I'm making things up, that I'm wrong and too sensitive, so I tell her it's a little scary to allow for the possibility that I am equipped to make decisions alone. In that solitude, there are so many voices whispering that I'm crazy, but now I wonder, how bad would it really be to be mad and safe? Does it matter if everyone else thinks you're insane if you're well and at peace? Is one of the sacrifices the self that I am in other people's eyes? What if I make it so that I only exist in my own gaze?

As my visibility has increased, my needs around safety have changed quickly enough to leave me disoriented. I know I'm not alone. I've been watching other people ascend at a steady and plotted speed, after years and years of doing the work, and I've seen their shock at the betrayals that came with that. My reaction to this accumulation of power or shine or whatever we want to call it is to retreat. I am a bruise and people are rough. I might have always been a bruise and just lost the capacity to pretend to be anything else.

I moved to the swamp so I could disappear a little. New York was too much; I couldn't leave home without worrying about being recognized. The first week in my last apartment there, I got recognized while walking to the Rite Aid on the corner, wearing an ankle-length winter coat. Once **Freshwater** came out, the list of places in the city became long and random: while checking out at the Whole Foods on Houston, while biking through SoHo, while having an intimate conversation with my best friend on the L train. Once, a woman followed me into a nail salon to confront me about an interview that my agents had canceled with the magazine that hired her, accusing me of standing her up. I'd never even corresponded with her; I'm not the one who sets up my meetings. I remember standing there with a bottle of nail polish in my hand, listening to her tell me how she saw me on the street and decided to follow me into the salon, and all I could think was that I was only in town for twenty-four hours, I was sick and exhausted, and the last thing I needed was to suddenly slap on the mask of my public persona to placate a complete stranger. I should have told her to leave me the fuck alone, but that would have been a whole thing, so I played along apologetically until she left. I swear, at some point when all people can see is your public persona, you stop being a person. I'm writing this letter to you because it's invaluable to not feel alone when thousands of eyes are watching.

I used to think I wanted to be famous. Now I think I just want to be safe, with enough resources to build even more safety around myself. Embodiment is war, in a sense. At some point, everyone is capable of snarling at you with nothing in their head past survival; you just have to back them into the right corners, to see it roar forward. Something about this kind of visibility does feel like a corner, even if it looks like wings to everyone else. There is so much that's unseen: the way it feels to never know who's watching you, the hesitation in speaking about it because there's always someone who thinks it's not that serious and you're not that big of a deal to be making this much of a fuss. The godforsaken isolation, the chasms that now stretch between you and everyone who doesn't want to admit your life has morphed into something neither of you quite recognize anymore, between you and those who want to use you, between you and those whose desires you can't quite read and therefore don't quite trust. I retreat from all of it because it's safer to just not gamble at all. I don't trust people, and masks can be adept things. I'm okay with being this guarded, whether other people agree that it's necessary or not. My therapist would be proud. I draw boundaries like scything fire, making a moat of flame around me; I am a dragon in a golden lair; I am inaccessible and unavailable.

Tamara teaches me about insulation, which is really a lesson about community. "You should never go anywhere alone," she says. Her family has been in Brooklyn for more than a hundred years; she tells me about her and her cousins insulating each other. On the night of the **Freshwater** launch, she met me outside with a green juice; she taught me how to take care of my flesh after expending such energy. In New York, either she or Alex come with me to readings, galas, and shoots. It makes such a difference, I am stunned. I tell my agents I won't travel without a companion coming with me or waiting at my destination. Ann meets me in LA; you meet me in San Francisco; Alex flies with me to Boston. When Tiona came to town and we did the NY Art Book Fair together, she gave me one of her anxiety gummies before we walked in. There were so many people there, it was ridiculous. She reached out to hold my hand as we walked, and I remember feeling proud that I could show up as her insulation, buffer her against the massed crowds pushing through the building. It was, I think, forty-eight hours after the magician had thrown me in the ring. I was fragile but I could be useful, and that is something that I think is important, to shield the people we care about. While Tiona and I were signing books, a mutual acquaintance delivered a photograph of myself with the magician. I was entirely too fragile to see his face unexpectedly, this poison of a love. Tamara had just been by our table. As soon as Tiona saw the photo, she took it away and called Tamara back. "You need to get rid of it," she told her, and Tamara took it without asking any questions. Later, I asked her what she did with it. "I threw it away," she said, unrepentant about not asking me first, unrepentant about protecting me. I loved her, and Tiona, very much for that. What is love if not a shield thrown up around you when you are too injured to throw it up yourself?

How far will we go to protect ourselves? I am fine-tuning all my shields, making a bubble around me that only vetted people can enter. Two years into my career, my team and I develop protocols. I communicate mostly through my agents—often, organizers have no way to reach me until I physically show up at events. When I have phone interviews, they send me the interviewer's number instead of sending them mine. I have two phones, four and a half numbers, unidentified calls are unanswered knocks on the door. I am not really here in the first place, too absent to reply to messages from strangers on social media, too much of a dragon to entertain people trying to bypass my agents. "We prefer more of a personal touch," one of them writes. "Working with agents can be a little tedious," another suggests. It makes no difference; the protocol is protocol for a reason. I'm not here. I am here and too much of a bruise. I put an out-of-reality message on my email, and for months I just don't take it off. I don't call my father, not even out of duty. I'm not here. I can't imagine becoming more present, only fading out more and more. Am I trying to become a ghost? Can I haunt my own home? Is that happiness?

Maybe all of this makes no sense; maybe it makes all the sense in the world. I don't care anymore. It's what I want, to be in a compound blocked out by tall bamboo and vines, have my people come and visit, write these books in the godhouse until the swamp takes us all. Maybe I'm being morbid since my heart was broken. I used to dream of traveling, and then I traveled and splintered along the way. Now, I'll do whatever it takes to feel safe. The dead magician doesn't have my heart, so I'm free. It's just a silly lifetime, it's just a few decades. If the doubters don't see how **hungry** people are, how they will reach and reach for you till there's nothing left, then they must be lucky to not know. I trusted people before, I thought they would understand when I kept telling them I was falling quiet because I wasn't okay, because my life was mutating too fast, too painfully, but then I saw how quickly people lash out when you restrict their access to you. It gets so ugly, this thing of punishing others for prioritizing their well-being over reassuring insecurities. I've been on the other side; I know that particular blindness. We can't save everyone; we might not be able to save anyone.

I gave a talk at Yale recently, and at the reception afterward, a woman told me about a paper she wrote on **Freshwater,** how she was taking it to a medical conference to argue for recognizing indigenous realities in treating people. It made me so happy, because it felt like a ripple, you know? You make one thing, and someone makes something else from that, and from there the world is changed, one fraction at a time. It reminded me that I send the work out as a proxy, which is part of the protection. The work is of me, but it's not me, and that's perfect because it can't hurt like me, it can't be broken or bruised. It's invincible, really—tens of thousands of copies swirling through the world, spells dripping into people. I've let that absolve me for not being able to do more myself, for the limitations of the flesh, the ways I couldn't afford to be a messenger crammed into planes, spreading this gospel with my own mouth. I'd rather be a dragon. I'd rather keep making the stories and sending them out like an army, waves and waves over the hills like a million monsters with salvation under their tongues.

All this has taught me to trust myself faster than I might have learned otherwise. No one else knows what is hunting us, what we are keeping at bay, what the constant onslaughts feel like or where they are coming from. It is only us and the fires we set between our homes and the encroaching dark, the rubber of a machete handle gripped against our lifelines.

We move.

Impermanence | Dear Kanninchen

Do you remember the café? There have been so many—we've said goodbye in about eighteen and three quarters of them. This time we were in Williamsburg, I think. The morning after the hotel. Was it the night before, when we sobbed in an alley? You can't breathe when you cry; globs of mucus crowd your passages and you always have to blow your nose. Your sadness was always choking that way. The alley was particularly abject, so I suggested a hotel. I used to think of glass windows in penthouses and your fantasies whenever I thought of hotels. I'd imagine us years from now, in KL or HCMC, pressed against the panes and still in love. (Are you still in love?) Now, when I think of hotels, I think of you lying to me in bed, in the Hilton that wasn't a Hilton. I think of you in my apartment, pacing as I ask you if you slept with her at your house. No, you said. At hers? No, you said, somewhere else. Where? A hotel room.

Looking back, I think you're lying, but this wasn't meant to be the point. I found a note you wrote for me in the café that morning. It was folded and browning in the suitcase I lived out of that year. It broke my heart as thoroughly as if my heart had been whole to start with.

You are loved. Right now. There is someone (me) building in their heart a house for you. This house is neither fictional nor imaginary. It is a place built around the things we share. Right now. It is the place where I feel like the opposite of

amputation . . . Terrors need time to quicken. We are a terror . . . I love you.

I wonder if we have been separate terrors to each other rather than a unit of terror scalding through the world. Today, in therapy, I had an epiphany, the kind of thing I would have texted you about afterward. I told my therapist about when we first fell in love, why I couldn't let you go, how my world cracked and bled every time I tried to. And you know I tried to. It would've been best for us, and I wanted so badly to do what was best for us. The only reason I don't beat myself up about it now is because you taught me it was okay not to be perfect, that I was still lovable even though I didn't know how to give you the space you needed without falling apart myself.

"It's better now, right?" I asked you, a week or two before we died.

You said a few words—ones I don't remember, because they were eclipsed by the ones that came after. "I can't say it's better now," you told me, "because I cannot fix my face to say it was ever bad." My magician, full of grace. We didn't know how to love each other well at first, but I thought we had forever to try.

My therapist's tiny curls are blond and tight to her skull. Her lipstick and nails are always impeccable. She crossed her legs and sipped some water from a steel cup with a straw in it. "All relationships end," she said, and it shouldn't have punched me in the chest the way that it did, but somehow there I was anyway, sitting on her couch with a stricken solar plexus. She kept talking, and I masked my face to look like a listening, but really I was turning the words over in my head, staring at their underbelly, trying to figure out why they cut so much. I remember the first time I realized someone could stop being your friend, when I was seventeen and in my sophomore year of college. My closest friend there was a Jamaican runner who could've been a model. She transferred to another school and was gone, just like that. I was so lost, so sad. I thought friendships lasted forever, like me and Chioma and Julie back home. We'd known each other since we were two, lived on Ekenna Avenue for fourteen years, and we were only separated when we had to leave for college. Even then I didn't think the distance would mean anything. I thought our bonds were immortal. I don't speak to either of them now, but I tried for a long time.

I am finding that embodiment is deeply traumatic, in no small part because of how it changes time. Imagine being ogbanje, like me. Imagine always being part of a cohort, unbound by the decay of flesh. Sixteen thousand years old, at an estimate. Maybe that's just where memory stops, or as far back as we can see. It's a measure of time that conveys timelessness while pretending to be finite. You are never alone. You are partnered with spirits like you, making small trips into bodies but always coming back. And then this embodiment happens, this violent birth ripping you away from home, and you aren't allowed to return. Instead, you're kept in a mortal form, subject to mortal rules (except for the ones you shatter, because you are still you). It's bad enough to be in an impermanent form, but the way time is corrupted goes much further than that. People don't know how to spin immortality. They are in violent flux; their bonds are

not like the bonds you have with your brothersisters. You keep learning and forgetting this
lesson, in wrenching directions. Your relationship with your human father ends. So does the
one with your human brother. The one with
your human mother is fraying. You thought
family was immortal, and they are not. People
die and keep being alive somewhere else,
away from you. You thought friendships were
immortal—never mind that you were a child
then. They are not.

We are still imagining together; all these
yous are me. I'm losing persons.

Impermanence is a cruel lesson to teach a
god. It says that something is not possible,
which doesn't make sense if you're a thing like
me, because of course everything is possible.
Have you tried bending the world to make
it happen? Oh, I forgot, your magic doesn't
stretch that far. No matter. Like I said, time
is corrupted here, and perhaps by corrupted,
I mean that it exists in the first place, what a
violence. It's made by measuring it, delineat-
ing it. Can you make a thing exist by caging
it? Does it only exist in the cage? If you destroy

the cage, what happens? Impermanence is a bastard outshoot of what humans have done to time. I keep forgetting that I'm in flesh, that it is slow and prone to injury, that so much of embodiment is defined by limits. Horrible, nasty little things, limits. Unnatural.

I wasn't meant to exist like this, but I am on assignment and since these humans have collared time and created ends, then this too will end and I will go home to my brother-sisters and it won't even feel like forever, because what is forever when there is no concept of anything else, a world with no end.

I keep forgetting.

"All relationships end," she said, and I flinched. I didn't know. I knew some ended, but in my head, I was holding out for a partnerspirit. I was waiting for an entity who would never leave me. I had learned to accept impermanence from other people: family, friends, a husband even. I knew the drill. Love them anyway; enjoy the time you have with them; just because it might end doesn't mean you have to be afraid. If anything, love them harder for that. But, I confess, I am terribly stubborn. Drag me into these human cells all you want; I still remember that I'm missing a cohort. I still believe I can bend the world into what I want. I have been trying to create immortality, bonds like the one I lost when I incarnated. I thought all I needed was another god. I thought you had enough power.

Every time I accepted impermanence with other people, I simply transferred the expectation of immortality to a partnerspirit who doesn't even exist yet. I see now how that might have been too heavy. Like I said, I forget the constraints of this world. It genuinely didn't occur to me that it was impossible until she told me they all end, and I thought, **Fuck.** She said it like a rule, you see, a rule of this world, and she was right. That's the whole fucking point of mortality, that there are ends. My god, the things these assholes have done with time. There are no forevers.

I forgot.

I thought I would find a partnerspirit and we would spin immortality, and to be honest, I thought they would die first, and I would die right after. That's as close as you can get to forever here, dying together. Afterward didn't matter, the consciousness that's been cobbled together in this body would be lost to oblivion. The dead ọgbanje goes home to its brothersisters. Playtime starts again, like it always does. There are forevers in our original world. I keep forgetting which world I'm in, one foot on the other side.

The note you wrote me is still full of hope, but it contains versions of us that are both ghosts now. I cry quietly in my bathroom so Katherine won't hear it. I want to try again with you. I don't know when to stop. I refuse the limits. I refuse the limits with you. But I am only a small god, put here by deities bigger than me, so I have to obey the limits, even as wrong as they feel. I still believe that if you worked with me, we could bend the world into anything we wanted. I wish you believed that too; it's the first step in worldbending. I can't believe for the both of us, and it makes me so angry and sad that you gave up. It's never too late—that's a human lie of time, there is no late, there is mostly now because now is so flexible, I find. You can change a whole life, a

whole world, inside of a now. The change can
be a ripple, but if you crack a whip and the tip
breaks the air of the future, the handle is still
in your hand now, don't you see? This is how
gods shape reality.

I thought you had enough power. I keep
forgetting.

That's why I couldn't let you go, my burning and crashing magician, because I expected
you to stay forever, so every time you stepped
away, my head went mad with abandonment.
The threat of an end, even a temporary one—
what does temporary mean, distance is distance, a bond severed is a bond severed, what
is this human back-and-forth, my cohort lived
in everlasting before the things done to time
gave that any meaning. I cannot survive the
thought of ends, of being alone. I accepted it
with other people like a trade. Fine, give me
these transient ones, but for the weight of
their fickleness, I will counterbalance with a
partnerspirit who will feed me immortality. I
think the humans would call that codepen-
dence, but that's because they have ends and
separations and all kinds of unnaturalness. I'm

not saying that's wrong. You have to bend to some of a world's rules, even if you bend worlds. There is an order to things, but I forgot.

I couldn't let you go because you were supposed to be immortal, with me. All relationships end, she said, and for the first time it occurred to me that perhaps I cannot bend immortality into this world the way I thought I could. There will be no everlasting partnerspirit, no embodied brothersister in this dimension re-creating the bond we had on the other side. These might be rules I can't break. It hadn't occurred to me; the impossible rarely does. I was terrified that I'd end up alone—but terrified because I thought the chance was slim, not that it didn't fucking exist. This is all so unbelievably heartbreaking, the way I've been waiting for an incarnation to find me. I can't tell you how many lifetimes of grief flashed through me, mournings stacked on mournings, shimmering and then dying because impossible things can't draw much of a breath. How could I forget that even if I'm not human, I'm still mortal, and that always means ends, many small deaths? Forever doesn't exist in this world. I thought you were forever; have I been breaking my own heart?

The other day, Eloghosa told me that nobody is coming to save us. I told her about the sadness I used to have with you. I'm sure you remember the thousand tearful times I wailed that you weren't coming to get me. I felt like a bedraggled kitten out in the rain, a child forgotten somewhere, that part of me that's stranded, abandoned, and **someone needs to come get me.** I used to trace it back to my human mother leaving us when I was eight, but I was wrong.

I was born, and no one's come to take me home. Embodiment is the stranding. I am marooned in flesh. I am alone, but I keep waiting for them to come and take me back, I keep trying to go home. They sent me out into the world, and I've fought it every step of the way, blubbering and trying to turn back. Thirty years, and I'm still trying to turn back. I'm still trying to burrow back into my mother's scales. I'm still trying to lie down in my father-husband's grave, tell him—pour the sand on me, pour the sand on me. Let me go home, let me come home. Don't make me go out there all alone. If I couldn't go home, I thought, maybe home would come to me, and home would be a god, home would be someone who would never leave, home would be a nonhuman who would spin immortality with me.

But I see now, especially after this last attempt to return, that I will go home eventually, yes, but first, I have a mission. I was sent here to do something, to make this work.

I can hear my brothersisters, exasperated beyond measure. It's a short term in the larger picture, they point out, just a few decades and then you can come home, but you keep turning away, you keep crying and trying to burrow back. You have to be brave, my love, they whisper, you have to move forward. You've called yourself a small god. It's time to be a big god now.

I can feel the instruction heavy on the back of my neck, the demand that I do my job. No one is coming to get me, but I'm walking toward them because home is at the end of this, home is in front of me, but I keep missing it because I keep looking back. Yes, they croon, that home is gone. It is a one-way trip, my love, you cannot undo being born, you cannot undo the body. There is no rush. It's okay for it to be slow; you only think it's slow because it's flesh. A few decades are nothing, they laugh. There's no need to destroy the body; the body is already destroying itself, the body is already dying. I take comfort in that. I am already being destroyed, I am already dying and going home, and I have work to do.

I wish I could claim my instructions were unclear, but they never are. My brothersisters are reliable messengers. Stay, they tell me, their voices overlapping. Look forward. Stop trying to run back to your parents. You'll end up in the place you're trying to find; you'll get everything you want. Give in to the flesh. The cage is not a cage. It is just metal. It is just armor that is already decaying. It is rusting, it is falling away. You are dying already. You are going home.

I know you are scared. I know you feel small and alone. We are here.

There's so much grief in me—about losing you, my magician; about mortality; about how wasteful it is for you to have been so afraid when you are just a few decades away from dying. What was the point of letting fear fuck up the little time you had left? It's fitting that you don't talk to me anymore. There might be other yous before me and others after, but you know the person you became when you started worshipping me, when you swore a future to me, swore a home and a heart, when I drew the sign of the cross on your forehead while you lay between my legs. That person is dead now, and I can't bring you back. We know the rules, they're the same across every reality: the dead can't come back. I wish you had let yourself be a god, because then that rule wouldn't apply, but the god I blindfolded by my bed, the god I loved, is dead—you killed him. I accept this end.

I have finally realized that in order to return to immortality, we must all die first. I look forward to it, and in the meantime it allows me to let you go, to bury you.

I leave New York and move my books and gold and clothes to the godhouse in the swamp. My apartment in Brooklyn looks so empty. Men like you have been breaking my heart in this city for ten years, and I think it's enough. I always try to make you gods and you always fail me so terribly; so be it. Your ghost can haunt this apartment all it likes, but without me here to remember you, to see your shade, I know it will fade. I have already forgotten what it felt like to make love to you, what your face looked like in pleasure. I will forget what it was like to lie with my head on your chest and your arms around me and your heart, your large and beautiful and lying heart, beating under my skull, reminding me that you are alive. All things end.

You are no different.

Opulence | Dear Kathleen

I think of opulence as a flaunting. On social media, I tag my photos as #theopulentogbanje, because this flaunting shouts that I am alive, that I wasn't cut into nonexistence. Something like me can exist in a contemporary context, loud and flashy.

Exposure used to be a threat for entities like me, but now I move freely. I still think of that McQueen quote as an instruction manual: **I didn't care what people thought of me, I didn't care what I thought of myself.** It is liberation, something to celebrate. I am learning how to be a big god, how to present as a full and conglomerate self, how to radiate all the desire and pain and power I feel without folding it down, without dimming. I practice seeing myself primarily through my own eyes. I want to see how bright I can get, and I want to show it off because why not? This life is short. If we live in rooms full of mirrors, how glorious can we get?

I've started fitting into Shiny, the godhouse, with all its gold and velvet. It doesn't feel too big. It feels like just the right size for where I am now—a little smaller, in fact. I wish I had one or two more rooms: a library, another spare bedroom, an extra studio. It took me a few months to figure out how to stretch all the way into the square footage, but moving all my things from Brooklyn helped. Sometimes, when I have anxiety, I leave the master bedroom and sleep in the other bed, the one with the gold headboard. My assistant saw me walk out of it one morning and she was surprised, but I'm not sure why. They're both my rooms. Every room in this house is my room. I keep my toothbrushes in both bathrooms, I read on the pink daybed in the studio and dance in front of its mirror. I take work calls in the second bedroom and go over the pilot script with Tamara on Skype. I eat at the breakfast counter, at the dining table, off the gold C-table in the living room, off the burl wood tray in the master bedroom. It feels lavish, and for once I feel lavish, too. I don't feel swamped by the house anymore, lost in its walls and eight-foot doors. Ann was right; it was there for me to grow into.

Recently, I had to leave Shiny for a week to attend the National Book Awards. I have a soft spot for that gala. When I attended it for the first time in 2017, as my publisher's guest, **Freshwater** was coming out in three months, and I felt like a literary debutante. I wore a slinky red dress and an emerald stole and twisted my hair into large buns with thin twists falling into my face. I wanted to arrive with a splash, and I think I did. I know I had fun, at least. I ate tiny lemon tarts to my heart's content and thought, How much fun would it be if I could do this every year? Make a tradition of attending the ceremony—not just as a guest but as an honoree, surpassing whatever skin I'd worn the year before? It seemed like

a fun spell to manifest, not to mention an excuse to dress up and dance, and so far the spell
has worked for two years. In 2018 I attended
as one of the National Book Foundation's
5 Under 35 honorees, wearing an orange dress
made of holographic sequins, my hair slicked
back into a straight ponytail. I wanted to be a
light, a kaleidoscope seizing reflections from
all around the room. The following year I was
a National Book Award finalist for **Pet,** and I
wore a draped dress in chestnut brown with
heavy gold chains at my hips and neck, a gold
sculpture on my face, my hair washing down
my back. I felt and looked like a god, which
was the point.

Fashion is a game of skins I can play with,
because the body is the first masquerade.
Think about it, what do spirits need to move
in this world? A skin, whether it's made from
raffia or wood or fabric or mirrors or flesh.
With fashion, I get to customize the skins to
reflect the spirit within, and that often means
extravagant, bright colors and textures bursting across me. In this game, you are my favorite
playmate. You send me stylist suggestions—
nail art, links to the new colors released by

Common Projects, tangerine leather, because you know me. We both independently buy the same Adidas sneakers, the ones with the pink suede top and candy red bottoms. I send you pictures of the Prabal Gurung dress I should've bought, the caped chartreuse velvet with the slashed bodice, then pictures of the Prabal Gurung dress I did buy, folds of purple and pink sequins. We pick our favorites from each of Maki's collections.

I wish you'd been here when Tamara came with me to a shoot for **Elle** magazine. They painted my face heavily into perfection, pinned and fluffed out my hair; then Yashua Simmons dressed me in REDValentino, pink tulle wafting in clouds around me, before putting me in front of the camera. I loved that skin. When **Freshwater** first came out, after the **Vogue** spread, Chloe invited me to a dinner launching one of their collections and dressed me for it: a cream leather jacket, a frilled blouse, yellow snakeskin boots with metal buckles. Jason Wu invited me to sit front row at his show and I brought my thrifted full-length fur along. These were all glimpses: a private dinner for Malone Souliers, a photo shoot for i-D dressed in Maki Oh, another one for Kindred—not a lot, but enough. We're just starting; we'll see where it takes us.

The pieces aren't even the important part. What mattered was my willingness to wear them, to focus on true skins as much as my sixty-seven faces. It's a language, I think; it says something just like these words do. I had to learn to listen to myself; I'd spent so long listening to other people, wearing skins that they recommended or expected, shy about putting my own on. I was scared that they'd point and laugh, but there is a distance between trying to be something and being it. Time closes the gap. It's all a story about unfolding. The manual stays the same: to try until you can, to be bold and patient. People take a while to recognize a new face, but they will fall in line. You just have to hold out.

I experiment with new things because designing Shiny taught me to trust my taste. I'm excellent at interior design; I'm good at styling myself too, I think. I commission Inaurem to make me gold nose pieces, I combine them with flywing glasses from Godsomware, and

Laura Estrada loans me a face contour piece. We'll make something custom together later. The jewelry—sculptures, really—are flown in from London, Seoul, Los Angeles. I hire the makeup artist from the **Elle** shoot, Raina Zohny, and she comes to my hotel in Chelsea. We sit for hours, designing lush makeup looks together, her hands painting my face into a god's skin. Everything fits together the way I want it to; execution is always a thrill when it succeeds, and I watch the spell the visuals cast on social media. It's a long game; I want to see what the opulence will summon. When the week of performance is over, I fly back to Shiny, to a different kind of luxury.

I order a mustard linen duvet set and watch my expensive kitten play on my king bed. Vines trail across my pale pink kitchen walls, leaving smudges on the limewash. I pick rosemary from the garden and roast butternut squashes in homemade ghee. It feels surreal to be alone and not sad about it, as if my own light is keeping me company. I tear fresh basil every morning for breakfast and dry roses in blush bunches. I wake up without an alarm because I don't have to go to a job. I can stay in bed as long as I want, play with the kitten, read fantasy novels while eating fresh satsumas, boiling cinnamon till the whole house smells warm. Tamara and I jump on calls to talk about the script. I write a few paragraphs of my romance novel. I order sushi and binge-watch every baking show I can get my hands on. I am so fucking glad that I lived long enough to feel the world that I built for myself; I'm grateful for the work I did when I didn't feel like living, because it has wrapped me in this life now.

I am growing lemon balm out back for Katherine; she likes to use it for tea. I'm saving chocolate habaneros in the garden so you and I can make syrups when you arrive. There are haw flakes in the pantry for my sister, a pretty blue bowl on the kitchen counter for Alex to put their rings in when they wash their hands, and I got some new yellow place mats for when we do our little dinners again. Ann and I are going to make akara from scratch, Marguerite will teach me that shadowbeni recipe I'm obsessed with, and I have a signed first edition of

Toni Morrison's **Jazz** to surprise Tiona with
when she gets here. The richness I want is the
kind that can be shared, where we are all together and alive.

Isn't it wonderful?

Regeneration | Dear Ann

There's a story, from when I was little, about a child wearing a new shirt who falls down, scraping their elbow and ripping the shirt. When they see that the shirt is spoiled, they start crying. "Well yes, the shirt is ruined," their father says. "But look at the wonder of your elbow, of your body, that it can heal when the shirt cannot."

I think we often forget that our bodies can do this, that we are regenerating when we heal; it's a superpower, like Wolverine. A body closes wounds, it replaces cells—the latter so much that we don't even have the same body we had however many years ago. I take a great comfort in that, in knowing that the cells people touched when I didn't want them to no longer exist. I'm not the same person I was before.

Katherine comes to visit me at Shiny, and she's so **alive.** It's fascinating to watch how she moves through air, space, and time, like a whirlwind of rose petals and pink salt and candlewax and herbs and tea and soups and sketches and paint. We went through the plants and she noticed I was pruning them rather aggressively, so we talked about it. Katherine's very into sitting with imperfections, while I excise them as quickly as they appear. I became curious—what would it look like to let a leaf brown all the way, to let the plants be the one to drop it off, grow a new leaf on its own time, instead of me hurrying it along? It made me think about patience and what healing can look like—sitting with the browning parts, waiting for them to die, waiting for the old skin to slough off instead of ripping it apart. Maybe the skin underneath is too raw, too new. Maybe if I was more patient with certain deaths, I would be more ready for the lives that come after them.

And so I started thinking about sitting in the rot, in the decomposition, in the decay of things. I had an anxiety attack at a gala and hid in the bathroom, thinking about how rotten I felt inside, how the people who engage with me tend to be either intimidated by my brightness, not bothering to look beyond it, or to be interested in nothing but that brightness, like there's something else underneath repelling them, so they don't want to go too deep. I felt like the thing underneath was something rotten, something decaying and dark.

When I told you this, you said I was haunted. I didn't know what you meant. "You are someone who has seen darkness and been consumed by it, but who is not dark themselves," you explained. We were talking about grief and the reluctance humans have to look at something directly. I can't help but look at it, and not just look, but see it, point at it, ask them to look with me.

"People don't want to touch things that are dark," you told me. "It's not that something else or another person is haunting you. You are yourself a haunting thing."

When I told Katherine about the rot, she said compost was useful. It's making something. I thought about that some more. When I sit with the decaying skins of myself, I begin to allow that I don't have to be a carefully pruned and perfect thing. That the decomposition can be interesting to observe, a necessary stage in regeneration, like pus or removing necrotic tissue. I have to allow the old skin to become lax enough to slip it off. I could tear it myself, but I'm trying to step away from aggressive pruning. I'm very glad that I died and resurrected. I cannot emphasize enough how old that skin was, how much pain I was in, how badly I needed to molt it away. On the other side of it, I feel raw, certainly. Fresh colors, new scales.

Eloghosa told me the other day that living is new, different. You said that you had decided to live as well, and I wonder if the three of us at least are choosing life from different angles, but on roughly the same timeline. I think about life now as more of a loop, a cycle that includes a constant death, selves that are dying and being replaced, skins slipping on and off. In that constant death, you find a fuller kind of living. I'm interested in that, in how being a dead thing leaning into decomposition is also part of a story of regeneration, of newness, of living. Years ago, I had dinner with Okwui Okpokwasili. At the time I was looking for how to **be,** desperately so. She told me that my search was essentially pointless. I was looking for a map where there were no roads. What was happening was that a new planet was forming, land masses were breaking up to the surface, seas were boiling forth. There is no way to map something like this. There is just seeing what the planet has done every morning.

This is what this period of my life has felt like—a new planet forming—and I cannot tell if I am the one traversing the planet or if I am the planet myself, volcanoes erupting in my right shoulder, extinction happening along my thighs. What is clear is that it is constantly unfamiliar, that whatever pattern I could expect from myself, or my life, or my relationships has been violently upended, tossed around, impaled on a thousand possibilities. I have no idea what is going to happen in the next year or month or week or even the next few hours, something could come along and warp whatever I've just been settling into. I had to remind myself that, before I started writing letters to anyone, I was writing letters to myself; all of these are letters to myself. I was writing reminders because so much of this is a constant war against forgetting. This summer, when I talked to Marguerite after one of the brushes with death, she told me, "You write when you are most fragile, because you're changing from one form to another. These transformations and transmutations that take place—it has to be painful."

"Go deep," she said. "You're not going to drown because you're not a being that can drown."

One of the reminders was about how to navigate all this: the madness of having whatever steady life you had before ripped apart, of a new planet forming, of an unrecognizable world that leaves you scrambling for anything familiar, but it's all funhouse mirrors and broken masks and lies you didn't even know you were blindfolding yourself with and you're still grasping for a lifejacket, a map, a flashlight, a constellation that will tell you where to go, for how to hold on to yourself without going the wrong kind of mad. It all feels so terrible, even as wonders beat against you from the outside, even as your dreams aggressively come true, it all feels like being lost.

I wrote these letters to remind myself that there is always a hack. There is always something I can do, even if it is the smallest seed that will grow into something almost as unrecognizable as I am becoming. Usually, when I wake up, catapulted from the dream realm into this one, there's a moment of being untethered. It feels uncomfortable, like being lost, as if realities are hovering above me and I'm trying to figure out which ones to pull down, but I can't reach them. In that moment, sometimes I reach for old things because they're familiar. They feel like sanity, they feel like something known—but when we're coming from the places we're coming from, running from the things we're running from, it can be treacherous to choose something old, to try and crawl back into a dead skin, to try and revitalize what has rotted.

What do you do? What do you do when

your life turns into this breaking and resetting of bone, of spirit, of self, of reality? When
you're unfolding, when you're being called to
become the beast that you've known you are
yet been afraid of, when your wings are crack-
ing and snapping out with ugly cartilaginous
sounds and bloody membrane, when you're
screaming because it hurts to be and it hurts to
be seen and it hurts to look at yourself. People
are running from you and turning from you.
You die and come back to life and you go mad
and you find sanity on the other side. What
do you do? How do you survive it?

I've asked myself what I need to put down,
what old skin I keep trying to crawl back into.
I'm not a child anymore. I'm not an abandoned kitten on a porch, a bereft thing waiting for someone else to come get me. Those
old skins died in that hospital in LA, they died
with the magician, and I don't miss them. I
don't miss the person I was when I was loving
him, the way that love kept me uncertain and
begging and wanting beyond sense. I told myself that being loved by him was making me
more powerful, and maybe it did, for a while,
in some directions. It is better without him

now. When he and I first fell in love, I warned him that I wasn't the kind of person to stay out of despair, if things went bad. "You are the sixth person I've fallen for," I said. "I have no doubt that there can be a seventh."

That was a clear skin; it got flayed away in the months that followed, but now it is growing back, and that is the miracle of regeneration. There is redemption in growth. At my garden in Shiny, I started a lot of the plants from seed, but the okro plants were my favorite. They didn't need to be started indoors; I just tossed them out on the soil and watered them and watched them become whole plants. With seedlings, once the root system is established, they hit a vegetative stage. It's dazzling to watch, as they go from being so tentative, so fragile and easy to kill, to becoming strong. That's the moment when I stop worrying too much about them, the moment when they become their own thing. The most substantial growth of the plant happens in this stage, it makes leaves and stems and branches, it takes a deep breath to become what it intends to be. Eventually, it will make flowers and fruits and seeds, but this first establishing is crucial.

My okro plants became so big that I couldn't pull them out of the soil, not even with both hands. I think my own unfurling will be like that, old roots running deep, a steadiness that cannot be shifted, but right now, I have become my own thing.

After being tentative for so long, struggling to become a seed, to find soil that I could germinate in, to make cotyledons and true leaves and now, to be here with a planet being created both before my eyes and behind them, is an entire wonder. I am not going to die. I choose to be alive; I choose to let everything else go. It continues to be hard and heartbreaking, as sacrifices always are, but I spent so much of my life afraid of unfurling, afraid of all the things other people feared in me. There are only a few decades left before I go home; I don't want to waste them being folded. I am choosing the new life.

I don't know what it's going to look like, other than brilliant perhaps to the point of excruciation, but I intend to wake up every morning and find out.

Thank you for listening. I love you.

ACKNOWLEDGMENTS

My gratitude starts at the source. To Oga God, Chukwu, the everlasting Creator—it is only what You say that comes to pass. Who can tell God what to do? Agụ bata ọhịa, mgbada awara ọsọ. You are the flood that carries the bridge, the Great Masquerade who dresses and guides Themselves. You are the one who holds my life, have mercy, my stomach is pressed to the sand.

To my deitymother, Ala, the python with the world in her mouth. To my chi, who continues to say yes with the force of a god behind it.

To Yshwa, my chosen senior brother, the son of God with infinite faces, for your endless companionship. To the brothersisters, my beloved siblings, for the maelstrom of love you surround me in, on this plane and the other. To my fatherhusband, the Baron, for letting me live in your palm.

To the nonhumans—Ann Daramola, Eloghosa Osunde, and Jahra Wasasala. Thank you for holding the center with me. I love you to the ends of this embodiment and beyond.

To the spirit-touched humans—Katherine Agyemaa Agard, Tamara P. Carter, Kathleen Bomani, Marguerite Lucerne Agyeman Prempeh, and Daniel José Older. You have my heart. That a book like this can exist is thanks to your unwavering solidarity.

To all the readers who see this work for what it is, who are unfolding beasts that needed these stories, you are worth all the costs. Let the world scatter under your hands.

ABOUT THE AUTHOR

AKWAEKE EMEZI (they/them) is the author of **The Death of Vivek Oji,** which was a **New York Times** bestseller and a finalist for the PEN/ Jean Stein Book Award and the Los Angeles Times Book Prize; **Pet,** a National Book Award finalist; and **Freshwater,** named a **New York Times** Notable Book and shortlisted for the PEN/Hemingway Award, the New York Public Library Young Lions Fiction Award, the Lambda Literary Award, and the Center for Fiction's First Novel Prize. Selected as a 5 Under 35 honoree by the National Book Foundation, they are based in liminal spaces.

AKWAEKE.COM

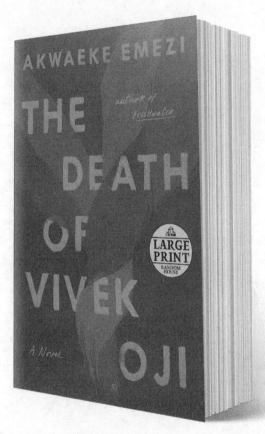